p

*F*AST FENG SHUI

9 Simple Principles for Transforming Your Life by Energizing Your Home

"*Fast Feng Shui* is a delightful book and filled with great tips and lots of positive affirmations. It is good for beginners and for advanced students. You can open it at any page and find useful information. I love this book!"

— LOUISE L. HAY
author, *You Can Heal Your Life*
and *Empowering Women*

"In the often complex world of feng shui, *Fast Feng Shui* is a breath of fresh air. Stephanie Roberts takes ancient concepts and makes them applicable to modern life in a way that is fun, valuable, and fast."

— DENISE LINN
author, *Feng Shui for the Soul*,
Sacred Space, and *Space Clearing*

"Creatively integrates your personality type and the power of intention with the basics of Western Feng Shui."

— JAMI LIN
internationally renowned Feng Shui expert,
instructor, and author

"Finally, a fun and easy-to-understand feng shui book that is logical, coherent, and user friendly.... I highly recommend this book to beginners as well as seasoned practitioners."

— ROBIN LENNON
author, *Home Design from the Inside Out*

"*Fast Feng Shui* is a fabulous, fun, smart, effective way to empower yourself and your environment and begin to attract and create the life you really want. It makes the mystical easy and accessible. Stephanie Roberts is brilliant!"

— SONIA CHOQUETTE, PhD
author, *Your Heart's Desire*, *True Balance*,
and *The Pyschic Pathway*

also by Stephanie Roberts:

Fast Feng Shui
FastFeng Shui for Prosperity
Fast Feng Shui for Singles
The Pocket Idiot's Guide to Feng Shui (Alpha Books)
The Clutter-Free Forever! Home Coaching Program
Clutter-Clearing from the Inside Out

FAST FENG SHUI
for

YOUR
HOME OFFICE

Creating a Workspace that Works for You

STEPHANIE ROBERTS

LOTUS POND PRESS, LLC

Published by **Lotus Pond Press, LLC**
415 Dairy Rd. #E-144, Kahului, HI 96732
www.lotuspondpress.com

"Fast Feng Shui" is a trademark of Lotus Pond Press, LLC

cover design LAKSHMI GRAPHICS *based on series format by* KATHI DUNN
main photo FLEUR SUIJTEN
inset photo ALFREDO PÉREZ BRAVO
author photo SHASTA ROSE

Fast Feng Shui for Your Home Office: Creating a Workspace That Works for You
by Stephanie Roberts

ISBN 10: 1-931383-10-3

ISBN 13: 978-1-931383-10-3

Library of Congress Control Number: 2006934428

this book is dedicated to

home based workers everywhere

and to my beloved husband

Taraka

who graciously shared his office

with me for many years

Contents

INTRODUCTION — 9
    A Brief (slightly biased) Overview of Feng Shui — 10
    What Feng Shui can Do for You — 17
    Envisioning Your Ideal Space — 19

CHAPTER 1. QUICK START — 23
    Home Office Assessment — 25
    Quick Fix Solutions — 32

CHAPTER 2. CHOOSING A GOOD OFFICE LOCATION — 43
    General Considerations — 47
    Unsuitable Spaces — 52
    Going by the *Ba Gua* — 56
        The Compass *Ba Gua* — 58
        The *Ba Gua* According to the "Mouth of *Chi*" — 62
        The *Ba Gua* and Your Occupation — 65
    Lucky Directions — 68
    Yin or Yang — 72
    Other Considerations — 75
    Putting it All Together — 79

CHAPTER 3. DEEP CLEANING FOR A FRESH START — 83
    Clearing Out Old Energy — 86
    The Problem with Clutter — 89
        Clutter and the *Ba Gua* — 92
    Good Housekeeping is Good Feng Shui — 101
    What's Paint Got to Do with It? — 106
        Colors and the *Ba Gua* — 110
        Color Selection Tips — 111

CHAPTER 4. FURNISHING YOUR OFFICE FOR
        GOOD FENG SHUI — 113
    Selecting Appropriate Furniture — 116
        Choosing Your Desk — 117
        Your Desk Chair — 123
    Desk Placement — 125
        Your Fortunate Sectors and Directions — 126
        Commanding Positions — 130

Avoiding *Sha Chi* 133
Weighing Your Options 143
Desk Position in a Mixed-Use Space 145
Ensuring a Good Flow of *Chi* 149
Your Office Door is a "Mouth of *Chi*" 150
Chi Flow Within Your Office 152

CHAPTER 5. REMEDIES AND CORRECTIONS 159
Office Location 162
Office *Chi* 166
Office Layout 168
Chi Flow 175

CHAPTER 6. ELEMENTS OF SUCCESS 181
Defining Your Aspirations 184
Finding Your Office Power Spots 193
The Five Elements and the *Ba Gua* 195
How the Elements Interact 196
Putting the Elements to Work 200
Activating Your Power Spots 205
The *Ba Gua* of Your Desk 218
Guas Within *Guas* 219
Focal Points 221
Final Check 222

CHAPTER 7. THE SECRET INGREDIENT 223
The "IVAG" Empowerment Process 228
Blessing Your Space 230
Embracing Change 234

APPENDIX 235
Drawing a Floor Plan 237
Defining the Compass Sectors 239
The Modern *Ba Gua* 248

Resources 258
Index 259
About the Author 263

Introduction

I have been happily self-employed since 1983—more than half my life now—working at first occasionally, then mostly, and at last entirely from home. Throughout the various stages of my working life I have enjoyed the many pleasures and have coped with the challenges of creating a home office that works for me. Whatever difficulties you may face in setting up a comfortable and efficient place to work in your home, there's a good chance I've confronted similar issues somewhere along the way from my first home office to my newest workspace.

Over the years I have worked at my dining table, in one end of the living room, in an alcove outside the kitchen, in a corner of my bedroom, and in a spare room taken over as office space. I've had desks that were too big and workspaces that were too small. I've suffered glare-induced headaches from unshaded windows and have experienced the pros (clothing optional) and cons (no view) of a windowless space. I have struggled to stay one step ahead of the clutter, have learned to resist the temptation to remain in pajamas all day, and from time to time have resorted to rearranging the furniture in an effort to break through writer's block.

When I began to study feng shui in the mid 1990s, I discovered specific reasons why some of my workspaces hadn't worked out very well in terms of comfort and productivity. And, as I used feng shui principles to redesign my home office, I discovered that my mood improved, my creativity flowed more freely, and I was able to get more done with less effort. Writing is not always easy, but it goes more quickly without the distractions and deterrents caused by poor feng shui. Your work will go more smoothly when your home office has better feng shui, too.

For the past few years—until just two months ago, in fact—I juggled the complexities of sharing a *very* small home office with my husband (who is my business partner and who also works full-time from home). As you can imagine, we were a little cramped, and that affected our productivity. Finding a private place in which to write the first draft of this book often meant grabbing the notebook computer and retreating to the lanai. As a workspace, the lanai lacked many standard office amenities, but the ocean view was inspiring and there was usually a nice breeze to temper the afternoon heat.

I am happy to report that we recently moved into much a larger home where I finally have an office of my own—quite a luxury after sharing a tiny office space for several years, and working at a desk in the living room for years before that. I have used the techniques and process described in this book to ensure that my new office is set up in the best space available in our house, and that it reflects my personal style, supports good work habits, inspires my creativity, and surrounds me with good feng shui.

As you read through the step-by-step instructions provided in this book, I will provide you with a thorough grounding in the principles of good feng shui so you can make the decisions that will best support you in working happily and successfully at home.

A Brief (slightly biased) Overview of Feng Shui

Feng shui (say "fung shway") is an ancient practice that originated in China thousands of years ago. Its earliest application was in selecting auspicious tomb sites, which was thought to ensure good fortune for the descendants of the deceased.

Over many centuries, this practice—which studied the interplay of natural landscape forms, water features, and wind patterns—evolved into guidelines for selecting auspicious dwelling places for the living as well, and for placement of key design features in the home, such as the entry, hearth, and sleeping quarters.

A number of different styles and methods of feng shui have evolved over the past millenia. Some very ancient methods are still practiced today, and modern approaches have evolved to meet the needs and expectations of a contemporary audience. This can be a source of great confusion to beginners, as the differences between the methods often outnumber their similarities.

Here's a quick summary of the major styles of feng shui you are likely to encounter as you read books and magazines and browse the Internet, along with my reasons for incorporating (or not) those methods into my own practice and writing.

The Stars Fly In

Feng shui professionals who say they practice "Traditional Chinese Feng Shui" are usually referring to the **Flying Stars** method. This practice uses an elaborate chart of numbers ("stars") calculated for a building based on the structure's compass orientation and year of construction. Some number patterns or combinations are thought to be especially auspicious. Others are thought to portend health, financial, marital, legal or other problems for the occupant.

Although this method doesn't have anything to do with real stars (the kind you see in the sky at night), I often think of it as being like a kind of astrology for the home. There's a basic chart based on the year and facing direction of the structure, as well as charts for the current year, month, and even day, should you care to get that detailed about it. Much of the analysis—as in astrology—involves how the annual and "natal" charts interact. What distinguishes this method from other popular forms of feng shui is that both space and time are included in the analysis.

The annual and monthly "stars" interact with the basic chart in positive, neutral, or negative ways. Various remedies are recommended for unfortunate star combinations to control or reduce their influence for whatever period of time that influence is active. Keeping up with these changes may be to your benefit, but most of us have many other demands on our time and attention, and good intentions are often not enough to ensure ongoing diligence in this area.

The Flyings Stars method does provide unique information that you won't get from other systems, which may or may not be helpful to you depending on your circumstances. For example, I always check the Flying Stars when consulting on a new construction project or when helping a client evaluate the pros and cons of a potential home. At this pre-move-in stage, it is easy enough to say, "No, that one isn't good," or to shift the planned siting of a future house to take advantage of a more auspicious orientation.

But what do you do if you live in an apartment, discover that it has inauspicious stars, and find out that the prescribed remedies include advice like "construct a hill in the back and place a water feature at the front of the property"? That's difficult to do when you live on the 14th floor, or if you are living in a rental property.

For those who don't know what year their home was built, or who cannot determine an accurate compass orientation, this method is not just unhelpful: it is literally useless. The Flying Stars charts for your home can only be calculated with accurate date and compass data. If you don't have those, you are out of luck, because this method will not be available to you.

If this is sounding a little more complex than you are prepared for, don't worry about it. The page and a half you've just read is all the Flying Stars feng shui you will encounter in this book.

Lucky Directions

The **Eight Mansions** method is another style of feng shui that uses the compass. In this practice, auspicious and unfortunate sectors of a home are defined by which of the eight directions the main entry faces: N, NE, E, SE, S, SW, W, and NW. Certain homes are thought to be more suitable than others for a particular occupant, based on that person's gender and year of birth.

Each individual also has **personal lucky and unlucky directions** (you'll find out what yours are in Chapter 2). This method of feng shui prescribes sleeping, sitting, working, cooking, and eating in a lucky sector of the home and/or facing a lucky direction.

In theory this is helpful stuff, but in reality it can be difficult to follow these recommendations while also meeting other requirements of good feng shui. Often, following the supposed "good" directions just isn't possible within the layout of the space you live in.

Placing your desk in a "lucky" location strictly by these rules, for example, may mean placing it in the kitchen or bedroom, or in the front hall, all inappropriate workspaces for any number of reasons. Facing a lucky direction while you work may require a desk position that breaks numerous other feng shui guidelines such as the ones you will learn in this book.

If you consult a book that teaches this method, you may encounter advice such as "the Six Devils sector is a good location for the kitchen, because the stove will burn up the evil influence." Unless you are building a custom-designed house or are prepared to engage in extensive renovations, this kind of recommendation is unlikely to be helpful.

The bottom line is that creating good feng shui in your home office (or in any space) usually requires making compromises and choices among the various options available, and in my experience the "lucky direction" options are often the first to go.

WHAT'S A MODERN COUPLE TO DO?

Another problem with the Eight Mansions method arises when more than one person shares a home or workspace. What do you do, for example, if your spouse's lucky directions are your unlucky ones, and *vice versa*?

In ancient China this wasn't much of a problem. For one thing, marriages were arranged based on compatible personal astrology. Where directions were an issue, the guideline was to give the husband's directions precedence.

These days most of us marry for love and worry about astrology later, if at all. And couples often share financial responsibility for their family. In deference to contemporary western culture and the emergence of the two-income couple as a norm, modern versions of this guideline state that the "main wage earner's" directions should be given precedence.

This adjustment of the rules is still less than supportive of families who rely on both incomes, regardless of whether one person makes more than the other, or who have a more enlightened attitude about the value of a home-maker's effort, whether paid or not.

In my own case, Eight Mansions feng shui says that my husband and I are fundamentally incompatible.* His lucky directions are my unlucky ones, and vice versa. Because we are equal partners in our business, there is no "main wage earner" in our household. There is simply no way to arrange a shared space according to these guidelines so it suits both of us.

THERE'S GOTTA BE A BETTER WAY

The real problem with both of these traditional methods—Flying Stars and Eight Mansions—is that most of us apply feng shui retroactively. We hear something about feng shui, are curious about it, and decide to learn more. Our hope is that we can make some improvements to the space we are already living in: a space that, for most of us, was not chosen with feng shui guidelines in mind.

The Flying Stars and Eight Mansions methods evolved to help you choose or build an auspicious house. On a very basic level, these are "thumbs up or thumbs down" methods: put your house data into the formula, and you get back a "favorable" or "unfavorable" verdict. It is assumed that if the verdict is "unfavorable" you will choose to live somewhere else.

Neither of these methods provides much in the way of advice about what to do if you've just signed a 30-year mortgage on a house and want to know what you can do to make the best of it, warts and all. As you will learn in Chapter 2, I do advise taking advantage of your personal lucky directions for your office—if you are able to do so—but there are simply too many drawbacks to the traditional methods for me to recommend them whole-heartedly.

---

* *Unfortunately, our perceived compatibility and happy marriage don't count for anything with this method—another reason why it's not my favorite style of feng shui!*

Feng Shui Adapts to a Contemporary Audience

Fortunately, just as cultures and societies have evolved over the centuries, feng shui has evolved as well. The contemporary method of feng shui which is the cornerstone of my practice provides principles and guidelines that are firmly grounded in the original, landscape-based methods (often referred to as "form school") but which are uniquely suited to contemporary use.

Contemporary Western feng shui focuses on creating a healthy flow of *chi* (vitality or life force energy) through a space. It addresses the need for a method that can be used where the compass-based rules of placement are difficult or impossible to follow. The most widely known contemporary method is the "Black Sect" or "Black Tibetan Buddhist" (**BTB**) practice introduced to America by Master Lin Yun. Most of the other schools of feng shui that have evolved in the U.S. are variations on the BTB teachings.

These modern practices are based on a map of "Life Aspirations," called the *ba gua*, that associates specific areas of the home with specific aspects of your life. Challenging layout issues and various forms of negative energy (*sha chi*) are identified and removed or neutralized. Remedies such as faceted crystal balls and wind chimes are placed to help welcome opportunities and encourage progress. Imagery such as paintings, photographs, and art objects is chosen and placed to enhance and reinforce the client's intention.

Another key feature of contemporary feng shui is its strong emphasis on the power of your intention to shift the energy of your home and initiate significant changes in your life. (You'll learn how to apply this important aspect of feng shui in Chapter 7.)

In this style of feng shui, the most important areas of your home (your "power spots") are determined not by the compass or a chart of numbers, but by what is most important to you at this moment in your life. This self-directed aspect of contemporary feng shui is a key ingredient in its popularity with modern users. Our culture has trained us to question authority and value self-determination, and these values are not always a good fit with the more traditional feng shui teachings, which tend toward dogmatic "shoulds" and "shouldn'ts."

Some traditionalists balk at this evolution, and insist that the Flying Stars method is "the only true feng shui." Others believe that the Eight Mansions method is the correct way to go. If you happen to agree with either of those opinions, this is not the book for you—but I hope you are more open-minded than that. Many practitioners today recognize that all methods of feng shui, both ancient and modern, contribute valuable aspects to the practice and develop a personal approach that blends ancient and modern wisdom.

Fast Feng Shui™ is my approach to teaching Contemporary Western feng shui. It is based on the BTB and form school teachings, and emphasizes the power of your intention to accelerate change. *Fast Feng Shui* grew out of requests from my clients, many of whom were frustrated by feng shui books filled with information that didn't apply to their home or situation.

Fast Feng Shui for Your Home Office closely duplicates the steps I follow in a consultation: analyzing the layout of the home, diagnosing problems, and prescribing appropriate adjustments. My approach to feng shui does not exclude the Flying Stars or Eight Mansions methods, but neither does it rely on them or give them primary emphasis. When dealing with interior spaces—which you will do as you analyze and make changes to your home office—it is my experience that the modern approach to feng shui offers a greater range of useful and appropriate options. The traditional methods then offer another layer of information that can be used to fine-tune your decisions.

In my previous *Fast Feng Shui* books, I focused on contemporary methods of practice. In this book you will learn how to incorporate your lucky directions into your own feng shui strategy in a way that will work for you.

Depending on your level of experience with feng shui, much of this information may be new to you, and you may be wondering how a 260-plus page book can have the word "fast" in its title. While you may not be able to get through all this information in an afternoon, I can promise you that what you learn here will help you get better results, faster, without a lot of wasted time or misdirected energy.

What Feng Shui Can Do for You

The basic premise of feng shui is that your life experience—your thoughts, feelings, and behavior, even the extent of your luck—is influenced by your surroundings. At the same time, the state of your home or work space is a reflection of your mood and attitude (which of course impact your experience as well).

A dark, dingy and untidy office, for example, contributes to an atmosphere of apathy and fatigue. This makes it harder for you to find the energy to make those sales calls or get the bookkeeping done, much less clean the place up.

Feng shui gives you the insight and incentive to become a mindful caretaker of your space. As a result, you live in greater harmony with your surroundings, and this helps you maintain a positive attitude and outlook. With feng shui, your home and office environments can better support you in achieving what you desire—in your career, your finances, and in all other aspects of your life.

Maintaining Appropriate Expectations

It's important to recognize that feng shui is not a substitute for good business practices on your part. Your ability and willingness to do your work well, fulfill your professional responsibilities, and be a good leader, manager, or entrepreneur, are also part of the total picture.

It's tempting to look at feng shui as being a little like a winning lottery ticket: "If I put my desk here and add this wealth symbol over there then my business will take off and the money will pour in." Well, it might. It's not uncommon for simple feng shui changes to trigger noticeable results. It's also quite common for people to use feng shui in hopes of a quick fix that will bring the results they want without their having to change or make an extra effort. This usually doesn't work out so well, even if things look a little better in the short term.

The bottom line is that feng shui is not a short-cut to success; it's a tool that can help you achieve a higher level of success more quickly.

Like most tools, it works best when used in combination with other tools, such as your perseverance, communication skills, leadership ability, and commitment to ethics and honesty in business.

Traditionally, feng shui is seen as one of five factors that influence a person's life. The other factors are your karma, luck, education, and actions, each of which may also contribute to the past, present, and future degree of your business success.

The impact of feng shui is most immediate when the difficulties you are experiencing are caused by poor feng shui in the first place. When other life factors are involved, feng shui can help you gain the perspective and insight necessary for setting appropriate priorities, making sound decisions, and taking effective action to get your business back on track.

Creating a Workspace That Works for You

In a traditional office setting, you have little or no control over key feng shui factors. Even an executive with a generous decorating budget for that prestigious corner office may be working in a space that is a feng shui nightmare. Lucky you: when you work at home—whether full- or part-time, whether as the boss of your own home-based business or as a home-based worker for someone else—you can do whatever you want with your workspace.

When you learn to think of your home office as a microcosm of your business, it becomes clear that this space deserves the same kind of care and thoughtful attention that you give to your business tasks and projects. Making conscious choices about your home office—where you set it up and how you arrange, furnish and decorate it—enables you to make more conscious choices about your business and your life.

This book will teach you how to use feng shui to create a home office that is not only functional for your business, but also uplifting to your spirit, inspiring to your creativity, and supportive of your long-term success.

Envisioning Your Ideal Space

Good feng shui doesn't just help you achieve more; it creates a space in which you feel more comfortable and where you can work with ease and concentration. What might that kind of space look and feel like for you?

What aspects of your current workspace do you appreciate and enjoy? Which distract, fatigue, overwhelm, or annoy you? Think in terms of both functionality and decorating style.

When dealing with a workspace we often focus on functionality, but every storage and decorating decision made (or not made) affects the style and energy of your office—and that has an effect on your work.

Imagine for a moment that you have a generous and unlimited decorating budget to spend on your home office in whatever way you wish. What might your space look like if you could furnish it any way you desired?

* Do you prefer energetic surroundings or quiet, sheltering spaces?

* Would you like a traditional look for your furnishings, or does a contemporary style appeal to you more?

* Do you prefer bright colors or neutral palettes, edgy modern or "shabby chic"?

* If you had a thousand extra dollars to spend on your home office, what would you buy first: a new computer; a new desk; art for the walls; a fabulous rug; more filing cabinets?

If you don't yet have a mental image of what your "dream" home office might look like, take a few minutes now to start to define what that would be for you. As you envision what your ideal workspace might look like, take full advantage of the luxury you have to escape the typical corporate environment's dull color schemes, plastic finishes, harsh lighting, and recycled air. Your home office is an opportunity to create a workspace that brings your own energy into balance and pleases your mind, body, and spirit.

ACTION STEPS

"Good feng shui" for your home office will affect:

- The **physical attributes** of the space: what you see, touch, and notice when you are in there.

- **How you feel** both physically and emotionally when you are in your home office.

- The **quality of work** you produce and the financial, professional, and personal results that you gain.

Complete each of the statements below to describe your ideal workspace. Examples of possible answers are shown below each statement; you may come up with something very different.

- **Physical attributes**:

    "My ideal home office is _____ , _____ , and _____ ."

    [spacious, airy, cozy, modern, quiet, bright, organized, etc.]

- **Physical/emotional states**:

    "When I am in my perfect home office, I feel _____ and _____ ."

    [calm, focused, energized, productive, competent, successful, inspired, etc.]

- **Quality of work**:

    "My perfect home office enables me to: _____ _____ ."

    ["double my income in the next 12 months," "complete my assignments easily and on schedule," "finally write that novel," "do a better job of building and coaching my downline," "have more time to spend with my family," etc.]

By the time you have finished this book, you will have made progress in all three of these areas.

Keeping a Feng Shui Journal

I recommend using a notebook or journal to record the insights and ideas that will come to you as you read this book. In the next chapter, you'll conduct a quick assessment of your current office condition, and learn what you can do to make immediate improvements. Write down what you learn in your journal, to make sure you follow through!

A journal or notebook will come in handy in Chapter 2, as well, when you'll follow a step-by-step process for choosing the best location for your home office. If your home allows few options, or you are simply too busy to change spaces right now, Chapter 2 will guide you through analyzing the benefits and challenges of your space.

Your journal doesn't have to be fancy, but it should be new, so it doesn't bring the energy of an old or unfinished project to your office feng shui plans. You'll learn more about the importance of getting rid of stale energy in Chapter 3.

Be prepared to really use your journal: stuff things in it, tear pages out, be creative. As soon as you start changing things around in your office—be prepared to move your furniture around as you progress through Chapter 4!—your own energy will start to shift as well. When you do feng shui, you are likely to find yourself more creative in all aspects of life, seeing things from new angles and having new ideas. Write them all down!

In Chapter 5 you'll be planning what cures and remedies to put in place; be sure to record your planned improvements and note what changes you experience as a result.

In Chapter 6 you'll explore the many ways to "activate your power spots." You'll want to have a notebook handy to write down your ideas.

Chapter 7 reveals the secret ingredient to making all of your feng shui plans and actions more effective. There's a role for your feng shui journal there as well, to keep note of the visualizations and affirmations that you'll employ to ensure your success.

1

Quick Start

Assessment & Solutions

*T*his chapter is designed to get you off to a fast start by helping you assess the feng shui of your current home office and suggesting some quick and easy improvements.

First, complete the **Home Office Assessment**. This will help you identify aspects of your home office environment that are supporting you or getting in the way of your success. Then, review the **Quick Fix Solutions** beginning on page 32 to find out how you can start to benefit from improved feng shui right away, while you take whatever time you need to learn and implement the ideas in the rest of the book.

Home Office Assessment

This Assessment will help you identify some of the good—and not so good—feng shui features of your in-home workspace. For each item below and on the following pages, circle the letter for the answer that most closely describes your home office.

1. **My desk is:**

   a) in good condition, and a good size; not so huge that I can't reach everything while seated, but big enough to hold my computer and phone and leave ample work space

   b) our old kitchen table or similar; we weren't using it anymore, so I figured it would make an okay desk

   c) a door on top of a couple of file cabinets

   d) also our dining room table

   e) a card table, or not big enough to be useful (even if it's a beautiful antique or reproduction)

   f) my lap

2. When I sit at my desk, the room entrance is ...

Your room layout may not match these diagrams exactly; pick the answer that best describes your desk position relative to the doorway:

a) in front of me, in the opposite corner of the room; I have a good view of the entire room and can see the door from where I sit

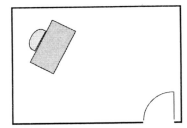

b) in front of me and to the side; I am not looking straight at the door, but can see it easily

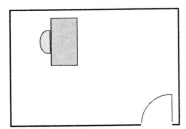

c) to the side; I am aware of it in my peripheral vision, but don't have a clear view of it unless I turn my head

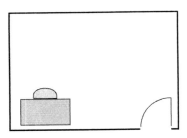

d) where I can't see it, but it is not directly behind me

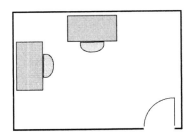

e) directly in front of me: I
    see straight out the door
    from my seat at the desk

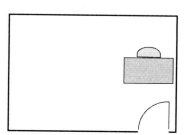

f) directly behind me

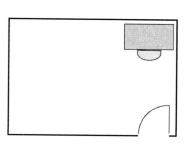

3. **When I am seated at my desk, I have my back to:**

a) a solid wall (no window)

b) a small window

c) a large window or sliding glass door

d) bookcases or shelves at close proximity

e) the rest of the room and/or the door

f) a corner wall or sharp angle:

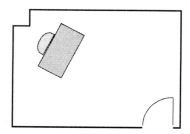

4. **My desk chair is:**

    a) my biggest office furnishings indulgence, one of those high-tech super-ergonomic wonders that cost more than I care to admit

    b) "executive-style" seating from an office furnishings store, with a high, padded back and adjustable height and tilt

    c) adequate, reasonably comfortable, purchased new, but nothing fancy

    d) an extra chair from our dining set; nice to look at, but not very comfortable for long work sessions

    e) an old kitchen chair (or equivalent) that I picked up at a garage sale or thrift shop—in pretty good shape, but not very comfortable for more than short work sessions

    f) old, rickety, unattractive, and uncomfortable

5. **When I look up from my desk or computer screen, what draws my attention is:**

    a) attractive artwork or a beautiful view of nature such as a nicely landscaped yard, trees, mountain or ocean view, etc.

    b) a photograph of someone I love or admire

    c) a view of an urban or manmade environment (other buildings, a brick wall, a concrete driveway or parking lot, etc.)

    d) a cluttered bulletin board or a clock

    e) a pile of work, files, unpaid bills, unfinished crafts projects, laundry, etc.

    f) a blank wall

6. **My office décor includes:**

    a) healthy live plants or an arrangement of fresh flowers

    b) at least one lifelike artificial plant or floral arrangement

    c) artwork representing plants, trees, or flowers

    d) dried flower arrangements, or neglected and unhealthy house plants

   e)   no plants or flowers in any form

   f)   an increasingly funky-smelling vase of dead flowers that I've
        been meaning to do something about for a week

7. **The oldest unopened mail (or unread email) in my office has
   been there for:**

   a)   24 hours

   b)   3 days

   c)   a week

   d)   a month

   e)   longer

   f)   since the last ice age

8. **The last time anyone dusted the ceiling fan or washed the
   windows in here was:**

   a)   within the past two weeks

   b)   sometime this month

   c)   a couple of months ago

   d)   I'm sure it hasn't been more than six months

   e)   it was clean when I moved in

   f)   to the best of my knowledge, never

9. **When I enter my home office on a typical day, it is:**

   a)   clean, tidy, and well-organized

   b)   basically tidy, with some papers or projects not put away

   c)   a bit of a mess, but I could tidy it up in less than an hour

   d)   messy, but I can usually find what I need without too much
        hassle

   e)   discouraging; I spend too much time looking for things

   f)   overwhelming; I'm never going to get control of the mess

10. My office lighting is:

    a)   adequate natural light for most daytime tasks, with good general illumination (*e.g.*, ceiling fixture) at night and excellent task lighting where I need it

    b)   pretty good most of the time; a little more natural light during the day and/or better task lighting at night would be nice, but it doesn't affect my work much

    c)   sometimes good—*i.e.*, excellent during the day, but not at night, or good at night but too much glare in the afternoons

    d)   adequate overall and task lighting, but no natural light

    e)   fluorescent only, but not too much glare or harsh shadows on my work areas

    f)   awful: flourescscent, with little or no natural light, and inadequate task lighting

11. What I like best about working at home is:

    a)   autonomy, being my own boss

    b)   flexible hours that suit my lifestyle

    c)   every day is "casual Friday"

    d)   I can play as much computer solitaire as I want

    e)   staying in my PJs all day

    f)   not bothering to shower or shave unless I have to go out

12. When I am in my home office, I usually feel:

    a)   comfortable, alert, focused, and inspired

    b)   competent and professional

    c)   a little stressed or distracted, but basically capable of accomplishing what I have to get done

    d)   unfocused; worried that I'm not getting enough done but somehow unable to be productive

    e)   stressed and anxious or bored, uninspired, or sleepy

    f)   like getting out of there as soon as I can

Scoring

Count up your number of answers for each letter (*a, b, c,* etc.) and total your score as follows:

———— **a)** answers x **5** = ————

———— **b)** answers x **4** = ————

———— **c)** answers x **3** = ————

———— **d)** answers x **2** = ————

———— **e)** answers x **1** = ————

———— **f)** answers x **0** = ___0___

total points = [ ]

What your score means:

- **41-60 points:** Your high score indicates you've already made good decisions about how to furnish and use your home office. A few feng shui improvements in targeted areas and you will have an excellent work space that will help you reach an even higher level of professional, creative, and financial success.

- **21-40 points:** Your home office isn't going to win any feng shui awards, but it is meeting your basic needs. Probably there are a few things about it that irk you and that you would like to improve. With a little attention to correcting feng shui flaws, your home office can be a welcoming and efficient work space that you enjoy spending time in.

- **0-20 points:** If you are serious about working from home, you need a home office that works for you—and yours doesn't. It's probably difficult for you to focus, feel creative, or be as productive and efficient as you'd like to be in this space. Making some serious feng shui improvements to your work space should be your #1 priority!

Quick Fix Solutions

Here is a brief discussion of why each issue addressed in the **Home Office Assessment** is important, including recommendations for quick changes you can make that will improve your home office feng shui.

1. YOUR DESK

Why it's important: Your desk is a representation of self in the workspace. What you choose to use as a desk makes a statement about the value you place on yourself and on the work that you do. What is your desk saying about you? What is it saying about the value that you give to your work and how well you support your own success?

In feng shui terms, saving money by making do with an inadequate desk is false economizing, and will undermine your success in the long run. A desk that is too small or the wrong height will affect your ability to work efficiently. A desk that is so large you can't easily reach all areas of it can imply that you are overwhelmed by your job or that you don't measure up to the task of running your business.

Second-hand or antique desks are potentially problematic, especially if you don't know who they came from or what that person's business experience was like: if that person's business failed, or he or she got fired, you have brought the energy of that failure into your own business along with the furniture.

What you can do about it: The best solution is to get a better desk. That doesn't mean you have to spend a lot of money on an "executive" desk. Some of those were not designed with good feng shui in mind, and in many cases a dining table or kitchen table will do the job very well and with fewer feng shui drawbacks.

If finding a better desk is not an option at the moment, do at least move it higher up on your priority list. In the meantime, look for ways to improve the appearance and stability of whatever you are using as a desk right now. Perhaps a fresh coat of paint or varnish is in order, or you might use an attractive piece of fabric to cover a scratched and worn finish.

You'll learn more about feng shui guidelines for furniture selection in Chapter 4.

2. DESK POSITION

Why it's important: When you are visually in command of your space, you are symbolically in command of your work and your business.

The ideal placement of your desk within the office will put you in what is called the "command position." In the command position you face the doorway from a distance, and are a little off to the side rather than directly in front of it.

From the command position, you have a good view not only of the doorway—and of anyone coming through it—but also of the entire room.

A "commanding" view of the space is not the only consideration, however. You also want to avoid being directly in the path of *chi* (energy) coming in through the door.

Diagram **A** shows an excellent desk position: you can see the door but are not in the direct path of *chi* (gray arrow). **B** has a less commanding view of the entire room, but is still good.

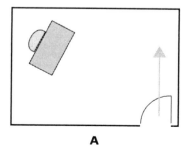

A

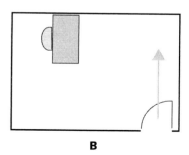

B

The positions shown in diagrams **C** and **D** have no command over the room or the doorway:

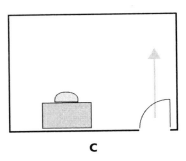

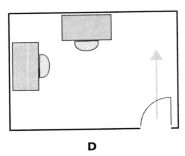

C   **D**

In the **D** positions, especially, it will be difficult to feel completely at ease and focused on your work. You are likely to be easily distracted by activity and noise outside the office, or startled by someone coming into the room.

In feng shui terms, having your back to the door places you in a position of vulnerability, regardless of whether or not you are in the path of *chi*. This is true even if you live or work alone and there is no one else in the house to distract or startle you.

Keep in mind that symbolic meaning is very important in feng shui. In other words, working in a vulnerable position in your office implies that you are also placing yourself in a vulnerable position in your career.

In the **E** and **F** positions you are overly exposed to *chi* coming in through the doorway, which can increase stress and anxiety and make it hard to concentrate:

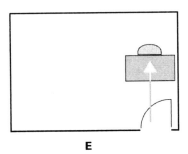

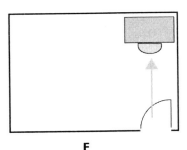

E   **F**

The **E** position does give you a view of the door, but here this is too much of a good thing. Your energy goes where your attention goes, so in this position your attention will be going right out the door every time you look up. You might discover that you get up and walk out of the room quite frequently. Even when you can keep your butt firmly planted in the chair, you probably won't be able to concentrate very well.

One situation in which the **E** position might be advantageous is if your attention is divided between work and keeping an eye on young children in a room nearby. It's not likely that you will get a great deal of focused work done in this position, but that's going to happen any time you mix work and child care, regardless of where you are sitting.

The **F** position is to be avoided if at all possible, as it has none of the advantages of the command position and places you in a highly vulnerable situation. In feng shui, sitting with your back to the door implies that you may be "stabbed in the back" in some way, such as by a colleague or competitor who takes credit for your best ideas, damages your reputation, or steals your clients.

What you can do about it: Angle or move your desk so that you can see the doorway from where you sit. If this is impossible, use a mirror to provide a reflected view of the doorway:

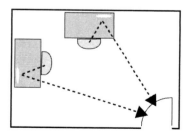

A mirror provides a reflected view of the doorway.

If you must place your desk directly in the line of *chi*, use a plant in front of the desk, or a crystal on the desktop to disrupt excessive energy before it reaches you:

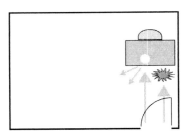

A crystal on the desktop deflects harmful *chi*;
a plant will absorb it.

3. BACK-UP

    Why it's important: A solid wall at your back offers both protection and support. A window behind you may indicate that your support is inadequate; the larger the window, the greater its impact will be.

    If your back is to the room you are at risk of being "stabbed in the back" by competitors or taken by surprise by developments in your industry or business.

    The edges of bookcases and shelves, or any sharp corner or angle, can be a source of *sha chi* (harmful energy). Proximity matters: the closer you are to the "secret arrows" caused by sharp edges and corners, the stronger their effect on you will be.

    What you can do about it: If you can't sit with your back to a solid wall, do what you can to improve the visual solidity of whatever's behind you. For example, close the curtains over a large window behind the desk, or sit in a chair with a high, solid back if you must have your back to the room.

    If you can't avoid exposure to a source of *sha chi*, try to move even a few inches farther away from it, or place something between it and you to act as a buffer.

    You'll learn more about sha chi, and what to do about it, in Chapters 4 and 5.

4.   SEATING

Why it's important: What you sit on represents the foundation of your business. When you desk chair is old, worn, wobbly, uncomfortable, or the wrong height for your desk, you and your business are functioning from an unstable or unsuitable foundation.

What you can do about it: Make it a priority to find something to sit on that is newer, cleaner, sturdier, or more comfortable.

5.   FOCAL POINT

Why it's important: The images, objects, and symbols you see on a daily basis have a strong effect on your subconscious. Images that you respond to with positive feelings help you feel good about yourself and your work. Anything that is visually depressing, discouraging, overwhelming, untidy, or unattractive will drag your mood and energy down if that's what you look at all day.

If your desk faces a blank wall, you are likely to feel blocked and frustrated in both work and life, whether you are consciously aware of those feelings or not.

What you can do about it: Pay attention to the focal points in your office, and make sure to place attractive and inspiring imagery where you will see it often.

6.   LIVING CHI

Why it's important: The natural world is composed of curving lines, uneven surfaces, and irregular angles; this is the kind of environment that mankind evolved in. The straight lines, flat planes, and 90-degree angles of man-made spaces are fundamentally unnatural. We feel more at ease when the hard edges and straight lines of our structures are softened or balanced with more natural shapes, with colors and patterns that evoke nature, and with the addition of nature itself in the form of plants and flowers. When you bring natural vitality, curves, and movement into your interior space, your own vitality is strengthened.

What you can do about it: Living plants and fresh flowers are excellent ways to bring natural vitality into your workspace. Good quality "lifelike" plants and/or artistic representations of nature are acceptable—though less powerful—alternatives.

7. COMMUNICATION

Why it's important: Unopened mail represents a disregard for the unknown. Regardless of the actual contents of the envelope or email message, any incoming communication that sits around unopened or unread for days (or longer) can indicate that you are ignoring opportunities or choosing to be "out of the loop" in terms of developments in your business or industry. Even bad news is best dealt with quickly.

What you can do about it: Get in the habit of opening your mail as it comes in and throwing out the envelopes, even if the only next step you take is to toss the contents in your in-box or stuff them in a "look at this later" file. Go through your inbox or "look at it later" file in more detail at least once a week and take action, file, or toss/delete permanently. Junk mail and junk email can be tossed or deleted without opening, but it should not be allowed to pile up on your desk or hard drive.

8. HOUSEKEEPING

Why it's important: Dirt, dust, and disarray are signs of stagnant or chaotic energy. The worse your housekeeping is, the worse the feng shui of your office will be, and the more difficult it will be for you to make professional and financial progress. Even the most feng-shui-perfect office layout and furnishings won't do you much good if you let the place devolve into chaos.

What you can do about it: Roll up your sleeves, grab a bottle of spray cleaner and a roll of paper towels, and get to work! Or hire someone to come in and do it for you. Start by cleaning up your power spots first (those areas of your office that are associated with your most pressing issues and goals; you'll learn where those are in Chapter 6) and then move on to the rest of the space.

9. ORGANIZATION

Why it's important: Clutter saps your energy, drags down your mood, and makes it difficult to get things done. A cluttered space is a space with poor feng shui. Plus, if you clog up your space with things that you don't really want, use, or need, there's no physical room available for new opportunities, experiences, and accomplishments to come in.

What you can do about it: Cluttering is a habit, and you can learn not to do it. Once you make getting rid of clutter a priority—and stop postponing the decisions that allowed the clutter to pile up in the first place—you will get a lot more done in all aspects of your business. Visit **ClutterFreeForever.com** if you need help.

10. LIGHTING

Why it's important: Light represents your ability to see your way in business and life. When your home office has poor lighting, your forward progress is likely to be low-wattage as well. A lack of natural light will sap your spirit, and the wrong lighting can strain your eyes and make it harder to work efficiently.

What you can do about it: Set up your desk and your task lighting to make it easier to see what you are working on. This may be as simple as closing the blinds over a window to protect against harsh afternoon sun, or moving your desk lamp to the other side of your desk so you can read your computer screen or papers more easily.

11. YOUR WORK HABITS

Why they are important: Working at home is no excuse for lapses of personal hygiene or slouching around in your pajamas all day. How you care for yourself is an indication of how you care for your business.

What you can do about them: There's a big difference between casual comfort and slovenliness. You don't have to dress for work or wear shoes if you don't want to, but changing out of your PJs into a clean pair of jeans and a fresh T-shirt marks the transition from at-home to at-work time and energy.

12. YOUR MOOD & ATTITUDE

Why they are important: How you feel in your space is a reliable indicator of whether or not that space is working for you. For example, if you are working full-time at home, but your "office" is shoe-horned into a corner of the basement, the inadequacy of that space devalues what you do. You may feel crabby and unappreciated no matter what great things you accomplish, because your surroundings do not reflect the significance of your work.

There is also a chicken-and-egg aspect to this, because *you* are one of the biggest influences on the energy of your space. If you hate what you do, you'll be miserable no matter what office you work in. The purpose of feng shui is to help you achieve greater levels of personal satisfaction, accomplishment, and fulfillment, and sometimes the biggest obstacle is inside you, not in your office.

What you can do about it: Approach feng shui as just one of many tools available to you for reaching greater success and accomplishment in all areas of life. Don't expect it to be a magic wand that will take care of all of your challenges without you having to learn, grow, or change along the way.

Applying feng shui to your home office is not a substitute for sound business practices, professional ethics, astute salesmanship, good customer service, or any of the many other human factors that support your success. Combined with them, however, it can help you reach your goals faster and more easily than you ever imagined.

Action Steps

1. Based on what you've learned from the **Home Office Assessment** and **Quick Fix Strategies,** pick three things you can do *right now* to improve the feng shui of your home office.

    For example: *open unread mail; move chair to the other side of the desk to face the door; bring in a better lamp from elsewhere in the house; water that plant on top of the file cabinet.*

    What are the three immediate actions you will take to improve the feng shui of your home office?

    *

    *

    *

    Now put this book down and go do them right now!

2. Indentify three steps toward improvement that you plan to take within the next 72 hours.

    For example: *shop for a new desk chair; arrange to have the carpet cleaned; catch up on filing, etc.*

    Be sure to include time in your schedule to actually do these things over the next few days:

    *

    *

    *

You're off to great start, and the journey has just begun. In the next chapter, we're going to look at what implications the location of your office within the home has for the success (or lack of success) of your business.

2

Choosing a
Good Office
Location

Location Analysis

As we consider the different factors involved in choosing the best location for your home office, it will help to have ready several copies of the floor plan for your home—reduced if necessary to fit on a standard size piece of paper. Make a few extra copies while you are at it, or set aside an unmarked floor plan so you can make more copies later if needed.

If you don't have a floor plan available, guidelines for drawing one can be found in the Appendix on page 237.

*I*magine for a moment that you have complete freedom to convert any room in your home into your office—without any complaints or arguments from other family members and without having to worry about where you will sleep if you decide to use the bedroom as your office...

Which room would you choose for your office?

Why?

What is it about that room that most appeals to you?

Perhaps the morning sun in the kitchen creates a warm and inviting atmosphere. Maybe the spacious dining room table reminds you how much you'd like to have a larger desk. It might be the tree-top view from the attic window that attracts your attention, the peace and quiet of the bedroom, or the wall of built-in bookcases in the family room.

Even in a small apartment that offers little flexibility in terms of workspace placement, take a look around and think about what parts of that space most appeal to you, and why.

The purpose of this exercise is to help clarify what features of a work space are important to you. There are many possible factors to consider when deciding where to locate your home office. Your own personal preferences are among them.

Your Home Office Deserves a Great Location

Most people have some kind of desk somewhere in their home, even if all it's ever used for is paying bills or writing the occasional greeting card. Too often people look around their home for a home office and plop down in whatever space is available, without considering whether there are other, better options. One very common mistake people make is to transition to working at home full time, without expanding or rethinking their at-home workspace.

Your home office is an important space, especially if you are starting a new business out of your home or are working at home full-time. That little desk in the alcove at the top of the stairs may have suited you just fine when you only used it for an hour a couple of times a week, but it's not an adequate home office (even if the builder labelled it "office" on your floor plan).

If the work that you do at home is important to your family's livelihood, your home office deserves the best possible location that you can find for it. That might mean rethinking conventional uses for your space, or negotiating with other family members to get use of a room that is currently being used for another purpose.

In this section of the book, you'll learn how to use feng shui guidelines to evaluate the pros and cons of potential office locations. If you have a choice of several different locations within your home, this section will help you to identify which one will suit you best from a feng shui perspective.

Perhaps you don't want to go through the upheaval of moving your office into another space at this time, even if that would be a better location for you. It's also possible that you live in a small home or apartment and have very little or even no choice about where to put your home office. That's okay. Sometimes you just have to make the best of what you've got, and feng shui will help you to do that.

If your home office is already set up in the only space available to you—or if you don't plan to change it—the information in this section will help you identify and understand the advantages and challenges of the space you're in. In the remaining sections of the book, you'll learn how to make the most of your office's good features, and how to minimize its less auspicious or less attractive aspects.

Choosing the best location for your office involves weighing and assessing many factors, which we will review in the remainder of this chapter. Much of this information may be new to you. Follow along as I walk you through each factor to consider, and take your time as you learn the new material. At the end of the chapter I'll recap the key factors and help you evaluate your options.

General Considerations

One of the biggest challenges to working at home is keeping your work from taking over your home life. Your office should be in a strong position in the home in order to best support your professional success, without being so emphasized that it overwhelms your family life.

We often think that working at home will enable us to spend more time with our families, but it's equally true that having your office in your home means it's harder to set work aside at the end of the day. Here are some points to keep in mind as you evaluate potential home office locations.

A Room of Your Own

It is best to have a separate, dedicated room—with a door you can close—to use as your office. A closeable door keeps distractions out while you are trying to work, and also helps you to "close up shop" at the end of the day so you can turn your attention to your family and personal life.

If the room you are considering or using for your office has an open entry—such as an archway—rather than a door, you may need to create a virtual door with a screen or curtains in order to adequately separate your work space from your living areas.

Multi-purpose rooms have mixed energies; in feng shui terms this means that if your office is in a room that is also used for other activities it will be harder for you to keep your mind on work, and you are likely to be less productive.

If you have no option but to use a portion of a multi-purpose space for your office, it will be important to create a visually separate and distinct work area in whatever ways you can. I'll talk more about this in Chapters 4 and 5, where you'll learn feng shui guidelines for furnishing and arranging your space.

Move Away From the Center

The central area of any space (whether a single room or your entire home) is like the hub of a wheel; it's the place where all the various parts of the space come together. In feng shui, this central area is called the *tai chi*. It is said that whatever is going on in the *tai chi* will affect all other areas of your home and affects all aspects of your life.

This means that if your office is in or very near the physical center of your home, every aspect of your home life will revolve around your work. For those who are single and very career-focused at this stage of their lives, that may not be a problem. If you are already struggling with life/work imbalance, however, having your home office in the *tai chi* is likely to add to your stress level.

The range of influence of the *tai chi* is a judgment call. The closer to the center you are, the stronger the influence will be; as you move away from the center, the *tai chi*'s influence gradually lessens. The influence of the *tai chi* will extend farther and be stronger in a space with a very open floor plan than it will in a space divided into separate rooms, as shown in the diagrams below:

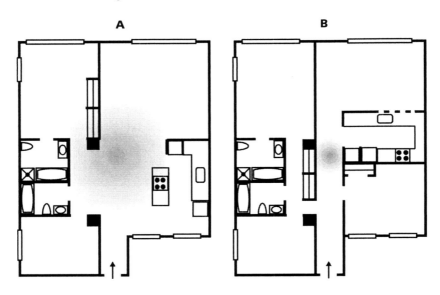

Apartment **A** has been divided into a 2-bedroom layout, with the kitchen and living areas remaining open and loft-like. The *tai chi* extends into the open space, as there are few walls to confine it. Apartment **B** has a 3-bedroom layout, with an enclosed kitchen, narrower hall, and smaller living room. This layout confines the *tai chi*'s influence to a smaller area.

An accurate floor plan for your home can be helpful in assessing how close your office may be to the center of the home. If you aren't sure how to find the exact center of your space, refer to pages 240-243 in the Appendix.

Proximity to the Front Door

The first room you see when entering the home is thought to have a strong effect on your overall experience. If your home office is close to the front door, this can lead to overemphasis on work at the expense of family. This is especially true if, on stepping through the front door, you see into the office and have a clear view of your desk, as shown in the first diagram, below:

A

B

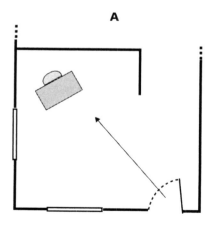
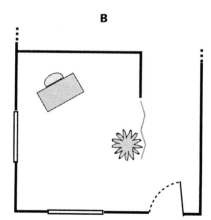

desk can be seen
from the front door

a screen and large plant
better define the space
and make the desk less
noticeable from the door,
without blocking the
view from the desk

If workaholic tendencies are adding to life/work stress, either choose a room further from the front door to be your office, or be sure to close the office door every time you leave the room.

If there's no physical door—if you enter through an open archway, for example—a screen, curtain, or large houseplant can help to create visual and physical separation of the space (see diagram **B** on the previous page).

Locations near the front door are not necessarily to be avoided, however. If you need to maintain strong connections with the outside world even though you are working from home—such as if you are in a sales or marketing profession—then an office close to the front door can be a plus for you. This position will give you a stronger relationship with the outside world than will an office in the back part of the house.

Those who require solitude and isolation (writers, for example) are best off in a location as distant from the front door as possible.

Front or Back of the House

From a feng shui perspective, rooms at the back of the house (relative to the front door) assert greater control over the household than do rooms in the front. If your home office is in the front of the house, with your family room behind the office, this can indicate that your children's schedules and needs will control (or even seriously disrupt) the work that you are trying to do at home.

This influence will be offset if the master bedroom is also in the back of the house, but if both the office and master bedroom are in the front of the house and the kids' spaces are in the back, parental control may be compromised.

The ideal situation for maintaining authority in the household puts your home office at the back of house on the ground floor, with the master bedroom at the back of the house on an upper level. Very few homes offer ideal feng shui, however, so don't be alarmed if your home layout makes an "ideal" setup impossible. There are ways to mitigate a poorly situated office, as you will learn in Chapter 5.

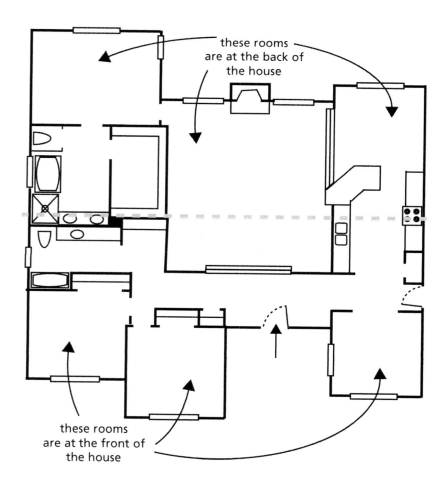

these rooms
are at the back of
the house

these rooms
are at the front of
the house

Client Access

If clients come to your home office, the more separation between home and business the better. It's best in this situation if your office has a separate exterior entrance, so clients don't have to walk through your family spaces to get to you. It will be harder for your clients to view you professionally if they've wandered through your kitchen or have had to negotiate an obstacle course of your kid's toys on their way to your office. Plus, you'll have to make an extra effort to keep those spaces clean and tidy; you shouldn't have to worry about doing the vacuuming during your work time.

Access to Facilities

Having a bathroom near your home office—so you don't have to wander off to other parts of the house when the need arises—can make a big difference to your productivity. If answering a call of nature takes you away from your office into other parts of the house, temptations and distractions will be harder to resist. You get up to take a quick bathroom break, and next thing you know you're watching cartoons with your five-year-old, rummaging in the kitchen for a snack, or putting a load of laundry in the washer.

Unsuitable Spaces

Some spaces are not well-suited for use as an office, regardless of their location in the home. Keep these considerations in mind as you evaluate your options:

Your Bedroom

The purpose of a bedroom is to provide you with a private space where you can relax, unwind, connect with an intimate partner, and—most important—get the sleep you need for optimum health and mental alertness. No matter what kind of work you do, the fact that it is "work" (rather than "play," even if you love it) means it doesn't belong in the bedroom.

Regardless of how well this room may meet the other feng shui criteria you'll be learning about in this chapter, it's not a good place for your office if you plan to continue using it as your bedroom. The presence of your workspace will interfere with your ability to get a good night's sleep, and the presence of your bed is likely to interfere with your ability to concentrate on your work.*

---

* These comments apply to adults' bedrooms only. Children are supposed to be learning as they grow, so it's okay to have a study desk in a child's bedroom.

If at all possible, either find another option for the office, or take over this room as your workspace and find another place to sleep.

Maybe you live in a tiny studio apartment, though, or enjoy an open floor plan loft that's all one big room, or there are other reasons why the bedroom is the only possible or reasonable place to set up your office. Recognize that your main challenge will be to create some kind of separation between the different uses of that space. We'll discuss this in more detail in Chapter 5.

Chi of the Space

Your home office should have good *chi* or "energy." Any space that is cluttered, dark, cramped, dingy, neglected, or generally unappealing does not have strong *chi* and will not be a good location for your office regardless of how well it meets other criteria.

You may be able to correct these problems with a good clutter clear-out, better lighting, some basic home maintenance or a fresh coat of paint. If not, cross these spaces off your list of options.

Upstairs, Downstairs

Attics and basements are usually not the best place for a home office, although in certain circumstances they may work well for you. If your greatest need is to be as far removed as possible from everything else going on in the house, then an attic or basement space may offer the privacy and quiet that you are looking for.

Keep the following points in mind as you weigh your options:

* In feng shui anything can be interpreted symbolically, and location is no exception. Attics, being at the top of the house, are associated with future aspirations. Basements, being underground, represent subconscious issues or situations from the past that continue to exert influence over our present emotional and physical circumstances.

Depending on your occupation, you may be able to use this to your advantage, such as having your office in the attic if you are a personal coach (helping others realize their dreams and ambitions), or by seeing therapy or counseling clients in your basement office (to better uncover the hidden influences driving their behavior).

- Attics are often poorly insulated, and may be brutally hot in the summer or bone-chillingly cold in the winter. Basements may be damp and cold or overheated and stuffy. Space heaters and air-conditioners can help, but are not ideal. Most office spaces have plenty of electro-magnetic (EMF) pollution already without adding more electrical appliances.

    Window air-conditioning units can be very noisy and distracting in a small space and will severely limit your options in terms of desk placement, as you will want to avoid sitting close to all that EMF radiation, noise, and cold draft.

    Some people are better able than others to ignore physical discomfort in order to get their job done. If you wilt or freeze easily and are distracted by even minor discomforts you will be better off in an area with better climate control.

- Good air quality and natural light—often lacking in attic or basement spaces—are very important to good feng shui. Lack of fresh air will affect your mood and energy and reduce your productivity. Windows that are too small, too low, too high, or non-existent will restrict your mental vision and make a strong and accurate "big picture" view of your work and life difficult.

- Headroom is essential for allowing your ideas to expand. The low ceilings typical of attic and basement spaces can inhibit creativity, contribute to depression and headaches, and keep you focused on the details of the present at the expense of forward thinking. A clear mind and positive attitude are worth making room for by choosing an office space with adequate ceiling height.

The **Action Steps** in this chapter are divided into two options, depending on your situation:

If You Know Your Location
Follow these action steps If you have no choice about where to place your office, or if you prefer not to move your office at this time. These actions steps will help you evaluate the pros and cons of your office location, so you can appropriately correct and/or enhance that space for optimal feng shui.

If You Are Choosing a Location
Follow these action steps if you have a choice of home office locations. These action steps will guide you through the process of evaluating the relative merits or drawbacks of the different spaces available to you.

If you will be sharing home office space with a spouse or partner, you should each complete your own set of Action Steps, and compare results at the end of the chapter.

Action Steps

If You Know Your Location
Based on the guidelines on pages 47-54, what are the advantages and/or disadvantages of your home office location?

If your location qualifies as an "unsuitable" space for any reason, what specific challenges do you most want to correct or address?

Record your answers in your feng shui notebook.

If You Are Choosing A Location
According to the guidelines on pages 47-54, what are the pros and cons of each space you are considering for your office? Write these down in your feng shui notebook.

Using the information on pages 52-54, can you eliminate any "unsuitable" spaces from your list of potential office sites?

Going By The Ba Gua

The *ba gua* (*ba* = eight; *gua* = area) is the feng shui map of the energetic influences in your space. It is a useful tool for evaluating the location of your home workspace. The *ba gua* is traditionally shown as an octagon with eight sections surrounding a central area: the *tai chi*. In the contemoporary styles of feng shui, we extend the corners of the *ba gua* to form a square, then divide it into nine equal sections:

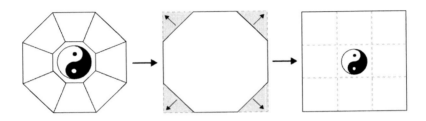

    The *ba gua* divides any space into these nine areas. There is a *ba gua* for your plot of land, a *ba gua* for your house or apartment, and a *ba gua* for each room within your home. There's even a *ba gua* for your desk.

Meanings of the Ba Gua

The *ba gua* is rich with meanings and associations. The meanings of the *guas* (sometimes referred to as "Life Aspirations") in the context of business are shown in the chart on the next page.

    You do not need to memorize the Chinese names, but they are a good reminder that each *gua* has multiple meanings. For example, many people think of *hsun gua* only as the "wealth area." A more accurate name for this *gua* is "Fortunate Blessings," which implies that prosperity and abundance are about more than just money.

    Hsun gua, by the way, is an excellent location for a home office, as it implies that the work you do there will not only bring in a lot of money but will also support non-financial aspects of success.

hsun **WEALTH** "Fortunate Blessings" Your income Financial well-being of your business	*li* **FAME** Your reputation and that of your business Industry rewards & recognition you receive	*kun* **RELATIONSHIPS** How well you get along with your business partner(s) Relationships with key customers & suppliers
jen **FAMILY / COMMUNITY** Your family Community involvement Your network	*tai chi* **HEALTH / BALANCE** How well you juggle work and family Your ability to handle stress	*dui* **CREATIVITY / CHILDREN** Your creativity Your employees or downline
ken **KNOWLEDGE** Keeping up-to-date in your profession/industry Self-awareness Your spiritual practice	*kan* **CAREER** What you do & how well you do it "Right Livelihood" Your life path	*chien* **HELPFUL FRIENDS / TRAVEL** Your mentors, support network, &/or upline Business travel

The Compass or the Doorway?

There are two methods for determining where the various areas of the *ba gua* are in a particular space. One method follows the compass directions. The other aligns the bottom row (*ken-kan-chien*) with the front door of the house without regard to the compass.

This can be a cause of great confusion to feng shui newcomers, because the information from one source will inevitably be contradicted in other sources. If you have read more than one book or magazine article about feng shui, you've probably encountered these inconsistencies yourself.

It is possible to make sense of all this, however. Let's take a closer look at each method before deciding which *guas* are where in your home...

The Compass Ba Gua

If you read a variety of feng shui books, you will encounter versions of the *ba gua* labeled according to the compass directions, with north at *kan* (career), and south at *li* (fame):

SE	S	SW
hsun **WEALTH**	*li* **FAME**	*kun* **RELATIONSHIPS**
jen **FAMILY /** **COMMUNITY**	*tai chi* **HEALTH /** **BALANCE**	*dui* **CREATIVITY /** **CHILDREN**
ken **KNOWLEDGE**	*kan* **CAREER**	*chien* **HELPFUL FRIENDS /** **TRAVEL**

E (left of middle row) · W (right of middle row)

NE — N — NW

CYCLES OF TIME

In the Chinese system north is shown at the bottom of the page, and south at the top, which is the opposite of how most of us in the West are accustomed to seeing maps.

This makes sense when you understand that cold, still energy settles; warm, active energy rises. **North**, at the bottom of the *ba gua*, is associated with winter, darkness, stillness, cold, and midnight. **East**, at the left side of the *ba gua*, is associated with spring, increasing light, warmth, growth, and morning. **South**, at the top, is associated with summer, brightness, movement, heat, and midday. **West**, on the right, is associated with autumn, lessening light, cooling, decay, and twilight. These compass directions make the *ba gua* a symbol of the daily and seasonal cycles of nature:

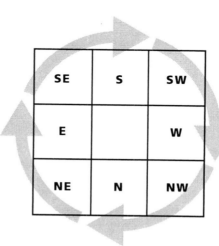

This alternative view of the compass looks upside-down if you're not used to thinking of north as being at the bottom of a map. You may find it easier to refer to this list instead:

SECTOR	GUA	MEANING
North	*kan*	**career**, life path
Northeast	*ken*	**knowledge**, self-understanding, spirituality
East	*jen*	**family**, community
Southeast	*hsun*	**wealth**, fortunate blessings
South	*li*	**fame**, reputation
Southwest	*kun*	**relationships**, business partnerships
West	*dui*	**creativity** & **children**, employees
Northwest	*chien*	**helpful friends** & **travel**

THE COMPASS SECTORS AND YOUR FLOOR PLAN

When the *ba gua* is defined by the compass directions, *kan gua*—the CAREER area—is assigned to the north sector of your home, regardless of whether that sector is in the front or the back, or left or right side of the house. *Li gua* (FAME) is the south sector of the house, and so on.

Some people use the nine-unit grid for the compass *ba gua* (with no direction assigned to the center). I mention this because you may see the *ba gua* shown this way in other feng shui books or in magazine articles. Using the grid for the compass directions is often just a "guesstimate,"and that can be a problem.

The house in the diagram below faces roughly SW, so the directions are assigned to the *ba gua* grid with SW at the front of the house (lower edge of the diagram), where the front door is:

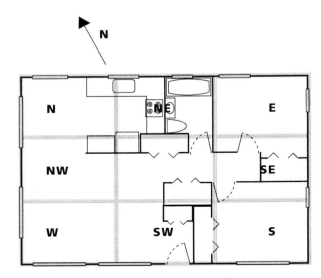

This house faces roughly SW, so the compass directions have been assigned to the *ba gua* grid with SW at the front door

The problem with this method is that most buildings—like this one—are not exactly lined up to one of the eight directions, so the grid method does not always depict the compass accurately. It is more appropriate to divide a space into eight 45° sectors if you want to use the compass to define the *ba gua*.

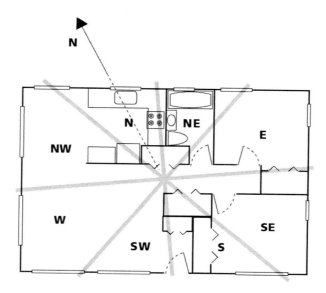

Compare the diagram above to the diagram on the previous page. You can see that the rooms at the top left and bottom right of the floor plan are mostly in the NW and SE sectors of the home, not N and S as shown by the grid method.

This could be a critical difference if you wish to use your personal "lucky" directions to help choose a location for your home office (as you will learn to do a little later on in this chapter).

I always use the eight-sector method—rather than the grid—when looking at the compass directions for feng shui purposes, and recommend that you do, too. Don't take the chance of *thinking* you're enjoing the advantages of a lucky direction, when really you might be under the influence of an unfortunate location!

Throughout this book, diagrams that show a floorplan divided into eight "pie-slice" wedges are illustrating the **compass** directions. With the exception of the "what not to do" example on the previous page, any diagram in this book that shows the grid style of *ba gua* is illustrating the modern, **doorway-based** method.

The Ba Gua According to the "Mouth of Chi"

The contemporary Western methods of feng shui ignore the compass directions and take a more experiential approach to defining which areas of the *ba gua* are where in any space.

The front door of your home (or of any space) is called the "mouth of *chi*" because *chi* comes into your home via the front door, just like you do. Modern feng shui uses this doorway to determine the placement of the *ba gua*.*

With this method, the bottom row of the *ba gua* (the KNOWLEDGE, CAREER, and HELPFUL FRIENDS areas) is at the front of the house, with WEALTH, FAME, and RELATIONSHIPS at the back:

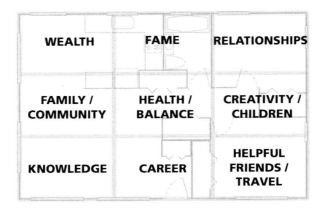

WEALTH	FAME	RELATIONSHIPS
FAMILY / COMMUNITY	HEALTH / BALANCE	CREATIVITY / CHILDREN
KNOWLEDGE	CAREER	HELPFUL FRIENDS / TRAVEL

By the way, there's a common misperception that orienting the *ba gua* "according to the entry" means that CAREER is always at the front door. This is *only* true where the main entry is in the *middle* of the front wall of the house, as shown here. Not all homes have the door in the center of the front wall. Depending on the location of your front door, you might step into the KNOWLEDGE or HELPFUL FRIENDS area instead.

---

* *The ba gua for your home is always placed according to the front door of the house—even if you usually go in and through the garage or a side door. Detailed instructions for using the doorway ba gua for your space can be found in the Appendix on pages 248-257.*

THE BA GUA AND HOW WE EXPERIENCE SPACE

I have a strong preference for the doorway-oriented *ba gua*, especially for interior spaces. That's because our immediate experience of any space (whether an entire building or just one room) is determined by how we enter and move through that space, not by wherever the compass sectors might be.

With this method, the CAREER area—which represents our path in life as well as the work that we do—is in the center of the wall through which we enter, with KNOWLEDGE and HELPFUL FRIENDS (those things that help us reach our goals) on either side of us where they provide the foundation for our progress (**A**):

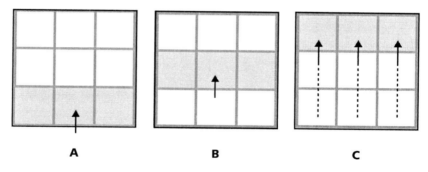

A **B** **C**

As we move into the space, FAMILY/COMMUNITY and CREATIVITY/CHILDREN are with us on either side, accompanying us on our journey. They challenge us to create an appropriate BALANCE between our professional and personal lives, so we can maintain our mental, physical and spiritual HEALTH (**B**).

WEALTH, FAME, and RELATIONSHIPS—the things that we aspire to in life—are on the far side of a space, beckoning us onward. We move toward these goals as we progress through the space (**C**).

Feng shui is about the impact of our space on our experience, so it makes sense to me that this key tool should be used experientially. The compass directions simply don't offer this kind of metaphysical correlation between the areas of influence in a space and how we move through that space

In spite of my preference for the doorway *ba gua*, I do also look at the compass directions to see what "flavor" they add to a space. For example, let's say the WEALTH area of your home (going by the doorway) is also in the west sector (CREATIVITY) according to the compass. That combination supports prospering through creativity: it's a good space for artists and writers. For less creative occupations, this location suggests that you could benefit from applying innovative techniques to your work.

If you have prior experience with feng shui, you may have a strong attachment to one method or the other. Some Actions Steps will ask you to look at your space from both perspectives, but if you feel more comfortable just using one method, that's okay, too.

ACTION STEPS

Take a few minutes now to determine the doorway and compass *ba guas* for your house or apartment.

Define the **doorway** *ba gua* first. Detailed instructions for how to do this are provided on pages 248-257 in the Appendix. (Many homes do not have a tidy rectangular shape, and the front door is not always flush with the front wall of the house. Second stories, porches, garages, etc., complicate matters further. Consult the Appendix to be sure you are accurately marking this version of the *ba gua* on your floorplan.)

On a separate copy of your floorplan, draw the *ba gua* for your home according to the **compass**. Instructions are provided on pages 239-247 of the Appendix.

The Ba Gua and Your Occupation

It is not essential to locate your home office in the WEALTH (*hsun gua*), CAREER (*kan gua*) or FAME (*li gua*) area, but if you can have your office in one of these favorable positions you gain additional support for overall success in your work. Other *guas* can be supportive, too, depending on the type of work that you do.

The table on the next page identifies specific *guas* that are especially supportive or relevant to a variety of occupations. There are two key factors to keep in mind as you review this information:

1) Some of the connections are made based on secondary meanings of the *guas* (that's why you will see the same *gua* defined in various ways in the column on the right).

    For example, we usually think of *kun gua*/SW—the RELATIONSHIPS area—as influencing our marriage or romantic involvements, but it is associated with business partnerships as well, and with maternal or nurturing activities.

2) There may be specific aspects of or circumstances surrounding your work that add to or change the suggestions presented here.

    For example, if you are a freelance writer, *kan gua* (associated with communication as well as CAREER) is the *gua* most closely associated with the type of work that you do. However, if you specialize in a particular field, such as parenting, health, or relationships, then other *guas* may also be relevant to your area of expertise.

    A novelist, on the other hand, might feel that *dui gua* (CREATIVITY) is most supportive of his or her work.

Use the information presented here as a general guide, and then think about what other *guas* may also be pertinent to your occupation and any specific focus or area of expertise within that field.

If your work involves	These *guas* are especially supportive		
Charitable work	Jen	E	Community
	Chien	NW	Helpful friends
Childcare	Dui	E	Children
	Kun	SW	Caretaking
Communications	Kan	N	Communication
Computer programming	Ken	NE	Knowledge
Counseling	Ken	NE	Self-Awareness
	Chien	NW	Mentoring
Dating & marriage services	Kun	SW	Relationships
Family counseling	Jen	E	Family
	Ken	NE	Self-Awareness
Financial planning	Hsun	SE	Wealth
Fundraising	Chien	NW	Helpful Friends
	Hsun	SE	Wealth
Graphic & creative arts	Dui	W	Creativity
Internet services/commerce	Kan	N	Communication
Law	Li	S	Reputation
	Ken	NE	Knowledge
Marketing/public relations	Kan	N	Communication
	Li	S	Fame & Reputation
Mathematics	Ken	NE	Knowledge
Ministry	Ken	NE	Spirituality
Network marketing	Jen	E	Community
	Li	S	Reputation
Personal coaching	Chien	NW	Mentoring
Publishing	Kan	N	Communication
Research	Ken	NE	Knowledge
Sales	Kun	SW	Customer Relationships
	Chien	NW	Networking
Teaching & tutoring	Ken	NE	Knowledge
	Dui	W	Children
Travel	Chien	NW	Travel
Wellness services	Kun	SW	Nurturing
Writing	Kan	N	Communication

ACTION STEPS

- Which *guas* are most relevant to the kind of work that you do (or will be doing) from your home office?

- Where are those *guas* on your floor plan according to the **doorway** *ba gua*?

- Where are those *guas* on your floor plan according to the **compass** *ba gua*?

If you know your location
Which aspects of your work are most supported by the location of your office?

If you are choosing a location
Are any of your potential office locations in supportive areas of the home, according to the doorway or compass *ba guas*?

Do any of the locations you are considering combine especially favorable *guas* when you look at both the compass *and* the doorway *ba gua*?

Also consider how other *guas* might support specific aspects of your work...

Rank your potential office locations according to the *ba gua*:

1.

2.

3.

Keep in mind that the correlation between the type of work you do and the various areas of the *ba gua* is just one of the factors we are exploring in this chapter. The area of your home that is best for your occupation might not be the best choice for your home office if it does not have good feng shui in general or meet other key criteria.

Lucky Directions

According to this feng shui theory, each person has four "lucky" and four "unlucky" directions. It is considered auspicious and supportive of personal and financial success if you are able place your desk in a fortunate sector, and sit facing a fortunate direction.

In general, I believe that a good arrangement of the furnishings in a space is more important than following your "lucky" or "unlucky" directions. However, it is nice to take advantage of lucky directions for your office—*if* you can do so without violating other principles of good feng shui.

Your lucky (and unlucky) directions are determined by your *kua** number, which is based on your gender and year of birth. That's birth year according to the Chinese solar calendar, by the way, so if you were born between January 1st and February 3rd, use the previous year to find your *kua* number.

There are multi-step formulas you can use to calculate your *kua* number, but I'm not going to include them here because it's much easier to just look it up in the table on the next page. If your birthday falls on Feb. 3rd, 4th, or 5th, you'll need to check the exact date of the Chinese solar new year to find out which Chinese year you were born in.

Or, enter your birth date into one of the many online *kua* number calculators you can find by Googling "kua number calculator."

---

* *"Kua" is an alternative spelling for "gua." In order to avoid confusion I use* **kua** *to refer to your personal number used to determine your lucky and unlucky directions, and* **gua** *to refer to the various areas of the ba gua.*

KUA NUMBERS

year	male	female	year	male	female	year	male	female
1930	7	8	1954	1	8	1978	4	2
1931	6	9	1955	9	6	1979	3	3
1932	2	1	1956	8	7	1980	2	4
1933	4	2	1957	7	8	1981	1	8
1934	3	3	1958	6	9	1982	9	6
1935	2	4	1959	2	1	1983	8	7
1936	1	8	1960	4	2	1984	7	8
1937	9	6	1961	3	3	1985	6	9
1938	8	7	1962	2	4	1986	2	1
1939	7	8	1963	1	8	1987	4	2
1940	6	9	1964	9	6	1988	3	3
1941	2	1	1965	8	7	1989	2	4
1942	4	2	1966	7	8	1990	1	8
1943	3	3	1967	6	9	1991	9	6
1944	2	4	1968	2	1	1992	8	7
1945	1	8	1969	4	2	1993	7	8
1946	9	6	1970	3	3	1994	6	9
1947	8	7	1971	2	4	1995	2	1
1948	7	8	1972	1	8	1996	4	2
1949	6	9	1973	9	6	1997	3	3
1950	2	1	1974	8	7	1998	2	4
1951	4	2	1975	7	8	1999	1	8
1952	3	3	1976	6	9	2000	9	6
1953	2	4	1977	2	1	2001	8	7

If you are curious about *kua* numbers for your children born after 2001, just continue the sequence for male or female *kua* numbers. Male numbers descend from 9 to 1, with "2" substituted for "5." Female numbers ascend from 1 to 9, with "8" substituted for "5."

Now that you know your *kua* number, look up your personal lucky and unlucky directions below.

These tables show "best," "good," "worst" and "unlucky" compass sectors for your home office based on your *kua* number.

Notice that the *kuas* are divided into "East" and "West" groups. All the *kua* numbers in each group share the same four lucky and four unlucky directions, although "best" and "worst" are different for each *kua* number.

LUCKY & UNLUCKY SECTORS FOR YOUR HOME OFFICE

EAST GROUP				
kua #	best	good	unlucky	worst
1	SE	S, E, N	W, NW, NE	SW
3	S	SE, N, E	SW, NE, SW	W
4	N	E, S, SE	NW, W, SW	NE
9	E	N, SE, S	NE, SW, W	NW

WEST GROUP				
kua #	best	good	unlucky	worst
2	NE	NW, W, SW	E, S, SE	N
6	W	SW, NE, NW	SE, N, E	S
7	NW	NE, SW, W	N, SE, S	E
8	SW	W, NW, NE	S, E, N	SE

This means that if you share your home (and home office) with a spouse or partner of the same group, you can more easily find locations that suit both of you. When an East group person and a West group person share a workspace, however, finding a space that suits you both can be a little more challenging.

ACTION STEPS

* Look at the copy of your floor plan that you marked with the compass *ba gua*, and find the sector that corresponds to your "best" direction. Mark this in some way, such as with a big star, or the word "best."

* Now find your three "also good" sectors. Mark these in some way, such as with smaller stars, or by outlining those sectors with a highlighter.

* Now find your "worst" sector. You'll want to be able to see at a glance that this is the sector to avoid if you can, so use an "X" or the universal "don't go there" symbol "⊘" to mark this one. The remaining unmarked sectors are your other "unlucky" directions.

If you know your location
Is your office in a "lucky" or "unlucky" sector? If you're stuck working in an "unlucky" part of the home for you, don't fret. There are ways you can make the best of the space by adjusting your desk placement, as you'll learn in Chapter 4.

If you are choosing a location
Look to see whether each of your office options is in a lucky or unlucky sector. Even if one of your options is in your "worst" sector, don't cross it off your list yet. An "unlucky" sector of the home can be okay for your home office if it has otherwise excellent feng shui, and if you set up your desk with care.

Although it's good to have your office in a lucky sector of the home if you can, it's not essential. Remember, this is just one of the several factors we are considering.

My own home office is in an unfavorable (but not "worst") sector of the house for me, but has generally good feng shui in all other ways, as well as other appealing qualities that make it the best choice of the several rooms I could have used for my office. I have positioned my desk so I am seated in a favorable sector within the room, facing a favorable direction. (You'll learn more about this in Chapter 4).

Yin or Yang?

What type of working environment do you prefer? Do you require quiet and privacy in order to concentrate, or do you work best in a lively environment that keeps you stimulated and alert? Take a few moments to think about the space you work in now as well as any other places where you have worked in the past. Where were you happiest, most comfortable, and most productive or successful? Where were you not at your best in thought, mood, energy level, or output?

See if you can identify specific physical aspects of your past and present workspaces that have either suited or defeated you. Be sure to base your evaluation on physical qualities of the space you were working in, not on a whether a demanding boss, challenging coworkers, or impossible clients made your life miserable.

For each pair of workspace characteristic listed below, place a checkmark in the appropriate column to indicate your preference:

INTERIOR DESIGN PREFERENCES

A		B
☐ Bright lighting	or	☐ Lower ambient lighting; task lights as needed
☐ Large or unshaded windows	or	☐ Shades or curtains
☐ Bright or bold colors	or	☐ Neutral or dark colors
☐ "Modern" decor	or	☐ Traditional, country, or "shabby chic" furnishings
☐ Bright, hard finishes/surfaces (glass, chrome, laminate)	or	☐ Upholstered furniture, leather, dark wood finishes
☐ Clean lines and crisp angles	or	☐ Floral or non-linear abstract patterns
☐ Wood or tiled floors	or	☐ Carpeting, or area rugs on a wood floor
☐ Everything out where you can see it	or	☐ Orderly and uncluttered; things filed away
☐ Shared workspace	or	☐ Privacy; a door you can close
☐ Activity, interaction	or	☐ Peace and quiet; no distractions

Look for a pattern to your answers. If most of your check marks are in the **A** column, you are most comfortable in a *yang* (bright, active) environment. If you checked off more choices in the **B** column, you prefer a more *yin* (calm, quiet, private) working environment.

WORK IN A SPACE THAT SUITS YOU

What does this have to do with your office location? Well, if you naturally work best in a *yin* environment, you probably will be happiest with your home office located in a quiet room that is removed from the hubbub of family activity and located on a side of the house that is protected from street and traffic noise.

If you function best in a more stimulating *yang* environment, however, you will probably work best in an office set up closer to the center of action, where you are aware of comings and goings both inside and outside the house, and where you won't feel isolated and alone.

If your answers indicate no strong *yin* or *yang* preference, then it's likely that you will be able to work comfortably in a variety of spaces in your home.

For those who do have a strong preference for one type of space over the other, this is a good time to think about which areas of your home will best suit that preference. Again, bright, active, noisy spaces are *yang*; darker, private, quiet spaces are *yin*.

Keep in mind that the balance of a room can be shifted—perhaps dramatically—from *yin* to *yang* or vice versa through changes to wall color, lighting, furnishings, and accessories:

* A small, dark room can be made to look larger and brighter with lighter wall color, large mirrors, and bright lighting

* A too bright, chaotic space can be made calmer and more restful with muted colors, areas rugs on a hardwood floor, and sheer curtains on bright windows

First evaluate which spaces in your home best suit your preference as they are now, without requiring a lot of redecorating or adjustments. Then consider whether you might be willing to make decor changes to adjust a space to better suit your preferences.

ACTION STEPS

If you know your location

- What qualities of your office suit your *yin/yang* preference? (quiet or stimulating, bright or soothing, private or public, etc.)

- What qualities of your office would you like to change? (too bright or too dark, too chaotic or unstimulating, etc.)

Note these preferences in your feng shui notebook so you can refer to them as you make furnishing decisions for your office.

If you are choosing a location
Think about each of your office options in terms of how well it meets your *yin/yang* preference.

- Which space will you be most comfortable working in, as it is now?

- Which spaces (if any) could be improved by changing color, lighting, and other accessories?

- How interested (or not) are you in investing some time/ effort/money in redecorating?

If none of your current options are a good match for your preference, and you aren't interested in investing time, attention, or money in redecorating, look for another area in the house that would be a pleasant place in which to work and consider whether it deserves a spot on your list.

Other Considerations

At this point you should have a pretty good idea of which parts of your home offer the most favorable locations for your home office or whether your chosen space is an auspicious or challenging location for you.

But we're not quite done so if your preliminary assessment has not yet resulted in a clear choice, that's okay. There are a few additional considerations to review that will help you make a final selection or understand more of the qualities of your current workspace.

ODDLY SHAPED SPACES

In feng shui terms, irregularly shaped spaces imply a higher than usual incidence of unexpected events. This is not necessarily a bad thing, unless you are someone who craves stability and hates surprises.

Whether you will be better off with your office in a "plain vanilla" rectangular room with four straight walls, 90-degree corners, and a flat ceiling depends on what kind of work you do and on your tolerance for chaos or need for stability, predictability, and order.

If you are not comfortable with change, surprises, or anything too unconventional (or if any hint of that in your work life could make your clients uneasy), it might be best not to set up your office in an oddly-shaped room, or one that has an irregular ceiling (such as an attic room with dormer windows).

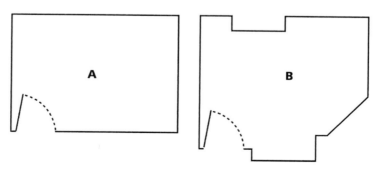

A is a better choice for stability and order.
B suits creative occupations and those who enjoy the unexpected.

An irregularly shaped room may suit you very well if you:

- Need lots of stimulation to prevent terminal boredom and too many on-the-job naps
- Are self-employed because you have a high need for autonomy
- Prefer each day to be different and not too tightly planned

You should be aware of two potential layout problems frequently found in irregularly shaped spaces:

- **Sha chi:** Sharp edges and corners can create "secret arrows" of *sha chi* (harmful energy) that increase stress and fatigue if you are exposed to them for long period of time.

  Irregularly shaped rooms may feature corners and angles that stick out into the space:

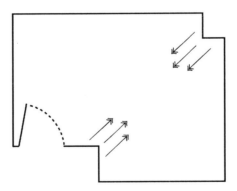

harmful "secret arrows" of *sha chi*
are a factor in this room layout

  The closer the angle or corner is to you, the greater the effect will be, so this could restrict possible desk placement, for example. (We'll explore the issue of *sha chi* in greater detail in Chapter 4.)

- **Missing areas:** The biggest drawback to an irregularly shaped room is that it may be "missing" key areas of the *ba gua*. If you are considering a space that is not rectangular, take a look at the *ba gua* of that particular room to see whether you have any missing areas or extensions in key *guas*.

For example, if increasing your income is your #1 priority, and one of your office options is missing *hsun gua* (WEALTH), that will be an important consideration for you.

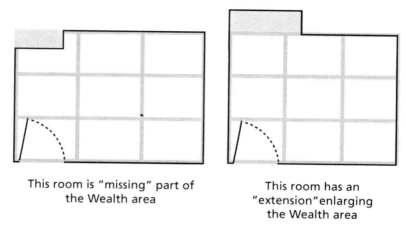

This room is "missing" part of the Wealth area

This room has an "extension" enlarging the Wealth area

THE "GOLDILOCKS" FACTOR

Some houses and converted loft spaces have enormous rooms. Using a room that is too large for your office can dwarf you. In feng shui terms, this means that you may feel unable to live up to the demands of your work, or that your business is out of your control.

On the other hand, if you are working in a room that is too small, you may feel limited in what you can accomplish or overwhelmed by your work. In the next section you'll learn more about the importance of allowing a free flow of *chi* through your space; for now just know that if you can't move easily around your office because the room is too small, you are likely to experience difficulty making forward progress in your career.

Make like Goldilocks and try to find a room to use as your office that is "just right" for you: not too big, not too small. This could mean making an unconventional trade-off. For example, in my previous home we used the master bedroom as our office and slept in the smaller bedroom. For us, this made sense; we needed less room for sleeping in than we did for running several businesses from home.

ACTION STEPS

If you know your location

* Does your office space have any irregularities (odd angles, corners) that may be "attacking" the room with *sha chi* or causing other challenges?

* Is the space an appropriate size for your needs, or is it too large or too small?

Make note of any concerns you may have about the room layout, so you can make appropriate adjustments or corrections (you'll learn how do to that in Chapter 5).

If you are choosing a location

* Review your office options in terms of room shape to see if any of those spaces present significant challenges (sharp angles or "missing" areas)

  Make note of these for future reference. If you do decide to a "challenged" space for your office, you'll want to apply appropriate remedies (coming up in Chapter 5).

* How does the size of each room you are considering fit your needs? Are any of the options you are considering significantly oversized, or potentially too small?

Putting it All Together

At this point you should have enough information to make a well-informed choice of the best home office location in your home, or gain a good understanding of the qualities of your current workspace. Here's a summary of pros and cons covered in this chapter:

ADVANTAGES	DISADVANTAGES
A private room of your own	Space is also used for other purposes
A door you can close	Open access (such as an archway)
Well-placed within the home	Poorly placed relative to entry, center, or midline of home
Separate entrance for client use	Clients have to pass through family areas to meet with you
Insulated from household activities	Exposes you to non-work distractions
Adequate headroom, lighting and ventilation	Low ceilings, no or few/small windows, poor air quality
Gua location supportive of your occupation/goals	*Gua* location not directly relevant to your occupation/goals
In a favorable compass sector for your *kua* number	In an "unlucky" sector for your *kua* number
Enables you to sit facing a fortunate direction	Forces you to sit facing an unlucky direction.
Suits your natural *yin/yang* preference	Environment is too sedate or over-stimulating
Room layout poses few or no potential problems	Room layout creates potential exposure to *sha chi*, or is missing a key *gua*
"Goldilocks approved" (right sized)	Space is either too cramped or too large

ACTION STEPS

If you know your location
Review your notes from the previous Action Steps in this chapter, and take a few minutes to compile a list of what you have learned about your home office's benefits and challenges.

If you are choosing a location
Review each of your potential home office locations according to the criteria listed on the previous page, and refer to your notes from the previous Actions Steps in this chapter.

The factors covered in this chapter are important considerations, but making the best choice for *you* is not just about weighing all the pros and cons of each space. It's important also to listen to your intuition. You might have a gut feeling that you will be happier and more productive in the room that by all other measures should be your second choice. If that's the case, listen to your gut.

It may help to spend a few minutes sitting quietly in each of your potential office spaces, even if you just need to decide between this or that end of the living room. Pay attention to your body and what it has to tell you. If you feel uncomfortable, unhappy, irritatable, antsy, or suddenly tired, these are clues that the room may not be good for your workspace.

If a best choice is not clear to you, consider asking a friend or family member for an opinion on which room will best suit you as an office. Often another pair of eyes might notice something you've overlooked, such as the fact that the laundry room is next door and noise from the washer and dryer might be intrusive, or that while the room itself is nice the view from the window is ugly and uninspiring.

Pay attention to the words they use to describe the space. Comments such as, "I don't know, it just feels depressing to me," deserve consideration. Ask for details, so you can determine whether or not the cause of discomfort is something that can easily be remedied (with fresh paint and better lighting, for example).

There's no reason to be concerned that if you make the wrong choice you will be doomed to failure. Feng shui is not just about picking a "good" space; it's also about making corrections and adjustments to improve any space, no matter what challenges it may represent.

If you still do not feel ready to make a final choice about which space is best for you to use for your office, table that decision until you have read through the rest of this book. Perhaps some of the ideas and issues discussed in upcoming chapters will help you make up your mind.

Don't be discouraged if even your best option only meets one or two of the possible positive criteria for a good office location, or if you are stuck in a space that is far from ideal. Feng shui is less about achieving a perfect space than it is about knowing how to make the best use of the space you are in. There are many ways you can use feng shui to create a better working environment, as you will learn throughout the rest of this book.

3

Deep Cleaning for a Fresh Start

*W*hen you step through the door of your home office, you should enter a clean, tidy, well organized space that is as attractive and comfortable as it is functional. Anything less will affect your mood, energy, and performance.

Everything in your office has an effect on the feng shui of that space. Before you arrange (or rearrange) your office furniture, you can ensure the best possible feng shui by first ridding your space of clutter and removing all other forms of stagnant, deteriorating, or disempowering energy. In this chapter you'll learn why it's so important to:

- Clear away any lingering "predecessor *chi*" that might be affecting your home office
- Make room for new opportunities and ideas by getting rid of clutter
- Get rid of the stale, stagnant energy of dust and grime
- Make sure everything is working as it should

I'll also review how to use feng shui to chose a new paint color for your office if you are planning to—or I can convince you to—repaint.

In the following chapters you'll learn how to select and arrange your furniture for good feng shui, choose appropriate remedies for less-than-great features of your space, and how to use accessories to adjust the *chi* of your office to create a comfortable and productive working environment.

Clearing Out Old Energy

If you've been working from the same space for more than a year, it's a good feng shui strategy to make as much of a fresh start as possible. The best way to begin is by removing everything from your workspace and staging it nearby. With the room emptied out, you can clean and refresh the space completely, before bringing back in only those things that truly deserve a place there and arranging them according to the guidelines you will learn in the next chapter.

If you are moving into a new home or converting a space previously used for another purpose into your office, you have a wonderful opportunity to follow this recommendation. If you just want to "tweak" your current office space for better feng shui you may think I've lost my mind to suggest this step (you're busy enough already, without taking on such a task, right?) ... but I'm recommending it anyway.

Taking the necessary time—and making the effort—to completely clear out your space before moving things back in may seem unnecessary or unreasonable, but I hope you will at least consider it. There are a number of advantages to this approach:

- You will significantly shift the energy of the space by taking everything out of it.

  Moving things is in itself a very good way to get stuck energy unstuck. The longer you have been using the space, the more you will notice the benefits of doing this.

- If you clear out all the furniture and stuff from your space, you'll be able to thoroughly clean the room before moving back in.

  If you are feeling a little less than inspired about your work or about the financial results of your work, a thorough cleaning of your office will help to "freshen up" the energy and inspire forward motion again. If you must leave furniture where it is and clean around it, the effect won't be as great although you will still reap some benefit.

- Psychologically you will feel as though you are making a fresh start.

  This helps you let go of mental frustrations and feelings of "I'm not doing as well as I'd hoped," or "building this business is taking longer than I thought," so you can get back to work with renewed enthusiasm.

- If the space was previously used for other purposes, you can more fully claim it as your own.

- You will see the room differently when it is emptied out, and may have some insights about how to make better use of the space.

  This can be especially helpful if your office shares a mixed-purpose room with other family activities. Moving everything out is a great opportunity to rethink how the entire space is being used.

- You are more likely to tackle the big jobs like painting the walls, moving the furniture around (which I hope you will be inspired to do in the next chapter), and cleaning or replacing the carpet, rather than putting these tasks off until "someday" arrives.

- You will see your furniture with fresh eyes as you move it, and may realize that you hate your file cabinet, or that your desk chair is looking very shabby these days and it might be time for a new one.

- As you go through the move-out/move-in process, you'll realize how much of the stuff you're hauling around is really clutter and that you can do without it.

Think about it. How long will it really take to do this? An afternoon, a weekend? The benefits you will reap over the next few months of improved mood and energy are worth the investment of a few hours —or even days—to make your home office the best it can be.

At the very least, if you can't do a total overhaul, devote some time to cleaning and getting rid of clutter. If you do nothing else, these two steps will dramatically improve the energy of your office. Here's an interesting exercise that will help you explore how in need of attention your workspace may be…

FIRST IMPRESSIONS

If you asked a friend or neighbor to come take a look at your home workspace—as it is *right now*, not after you've tidied up or redecorated—and give you an honest and unbiased opinion of it, what would they be likely to notice?

Is your home office neat and tidy and ready for business or is it cluttered and chaotic?

Is it so full of things unrelated to work that it doesn't look like a workspace at all?

Would your friend say, "Wow, you've got a great office!" or, "I can't believe you get anything done in here"?

Stand in the doorway or entry to your current home workspace and take a look at that space as though you are seeing it for the first time.

* What are the first three words that come to mind to describe your space:

* If this were a stranger's office, what insights might you gain from this room about the person who works here? What are three things you might assume about that person's work habits, priorities, or level of success:

* What do you *want* your home office to be saying about you?

The Problem with Clutter

Feng shui views clutter as synonymous with stuck or stagnant energy. The word "clutter" comes from an Old English word, *clott*, which means "to cause to become blocked or obscured." Like a blood clot that blocks circulation in a vein, clutter prevents *chi* (vitality or life force energy) from circulating through your office.

A visually cluttered and disorganized workspace saps your energy and erodes your spirit. It adds to your stress, slows you down and drains your physical, mental, emotional, and spiritual strength. It wastes your time, blocks your creativity, dulls your decisiveness, creates extra work, and makes you late for appointments.

Clutter nibbles away at your finances, one lost opportunity and late fee at a time. It erodes your composure. Clutter can keep you from reaching your goals and living out your dreams.

CLUTTER LEAVES NO ROOM FOR GROWTH

If that wasn't enough to inspire you to put this book down and go throw a few things out or clear the papers off your desk, consider this: an office filled with clutter makes it difficult to grow your business. It leaves no space for new ideas, new business opportunities, new client relationships, or new projects to flourish. (It will also prevent any special feng shui cures or remedies from working as well as they should.)

Getting rid of clutter is the single most important improvement you can make to the functionality of your office, and it should be the first item on your feng shui to-do list. This is especially true if you have been feeling stuck or uninspired about your work; getting rid of clutter is the fastest and most effective way to breathe new life and enthusiasm into your work experience.

If your business is not thriving as well as it should be and you aren't sure what's wrong, roll up your sleeves and get rid of any clutter in your office. Visible clutter on your desk, shelves, and in piles on the floor is a constant subtle distraction that keeps you from functioning at your best and contributes to the frustrations, wasted time, and increased stress of disorganization.

Closets and closed storage areas represent things that are hidden, unknown, or unrecognized. Hidden clutter in your office storage areas may be out of sight, but it stifles your ability to be intuitive and insightful. It can indicate problems that you may not be consciously aware of but which impede your success nonetheless.

Getting rid of clutter should be your first line of attack when you are frustrated by:

* Slow cash flow
* Difficulty attracting new clients
* Stalled or over-deadline projects
* Ineffective networking
* Feeling creatively blocked
* Missed opportunities and lost business

Make Room for Expansion

In long-established workspaces—whether in or outside the home—a common feng shui problem is overstuffed files and storage areas. When your hard drive, file drawers, bookcases, and storage cabinets are all full with many years' worth of accumulated stuff, there's no room for new energy (in the form of clients, cash flow, ideas, etc.) to come in.

Clearing the clutter out of your office is the fastest and surest way to make space for possibility. Not only will clutter-clearing dramatically improve your mood and energy, but it will also literally create space for your business (and profits!) to expand.

One of my first feng shui consultations was for a small business owner who was having trouble coping with changes in her marketplace. She recognized that her clients' needs were evolving, and that she needed to shift her business focus in order to maintain her current client base and attract new customers. She had ideas about how to do that and was excited about the new directions she wanted to take. But her business seemed to be stuck in a rut, and she was frustrated that her efforts weren't producing the kinds of results she'd expected.

When she invited me to assess her office, I immediately noticed that almost every wall in the office suite featured a framed memento of a past project or an award certificate or plaque that her company had earned. The problem was that none of this prominently displayed imagery was even remotely current; the most recent was almost ten years old. And all of it represented the kind of work she no longer wished to pursue.

Further exploration revealed that every one of her many file drawers was so overstuffed (some with files dating back over 15 years!) that it was difficult to retrieve or file anything. All the storage closets were full to capacity, and bookshelves were overloaded with reference books many of which were out of date. A brief conversation with her assistant revealed that the computer system crashed frequently due to an overloaded hard drive.

No wonder this energetic and accomplished business owner was having trouble shifting her business into a new direction: her office was so overloaded and stuck in the past there was literally no room for change or growth.

She admitted that she knew her office was ripe for a good de-cluttering, but that it hadn't seemed to be a good use of time and energy when there was so much else she wanted to get done. Unfortunately, all that clutter was a big reason why her new business initiatives weren't producing results.

CLUTTER CLEARING HELPS YOU LET GO OF THE PAST

How can you move forward when your space is stuck in the past? Take a look around your office to see how much stuff you are holding on to from past jobs and career paths. Clear that stuff out, and you create room for growth in a new direction.

Clearing out your office isn't just about doing housework and catching up on the filing; it's about creating space in your psyche for the next phase of growth by freeing yourself from the past and shaking off feelings of powerlessness.

When your office is de-cluttered, you can consciously choose to surround yourself with things that nourish your soul and support you in your life's work.

Clutter and the Ba Gua

In the previous chapter, you learned about the feng shui *ba gua*—the "energy map" of your space. The *ba gua* can be used for any defined area; there is a *ba gua* for your entire home and also a *ba gua* for each room within your home, including your office.*

Here's how clutter in the various *guas* within your office could be affecting you and your business:

Clutter in the **CAREER** area (*kan gua*) "muddies the water" and can result in:

- Unclear or misunderstood communications going out from your office

- Feeling unsure what role you wish to take in your profession

- People contacting you because they misperceive your role or services; you waste time clarifying what you do and directing them elsewhere for assistance

Clearing clutter here will help you build a successful career doing what you love, rather than what other people think you should do.

Clutter in the **KNOWLEDGE** area (*ken gua*) can make it hard to:

- Stay current with new developments in your field

- Get accurate information when you need it

- Have a clear understanding of your personal needs and priorities

  Clearing clutter here will make it easier for you to make appropriate decisions that support both your professional success and your personal growth and happiness.

---

* *To determine how the ba gua fits your office, use the guidelines on page 257 for the doorway method.*

 Clutter in the **FAMILY / COMMUNITY** area (*jen gua*) can make it difficult to:

- Get new projects started (this area governs fresh starts of all kinds)
- Attract new members to your network marketing "family"
- Gain community support for your business
- Make time for family commitments

Clearing clutter here will help you balance family and work commitments and expand your community/network connections.

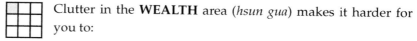 Clutter in the **WEALTH** area (*hsun gua*) makes it harder for you to:

- Prosper financially
- Increase your cash flow
- Increase your profits
- Attract new income opportunities
- Resolve financial disputes
- Have a clear understanding of your financial situation

Clearing clutter here will help you make more money faster, better manage your expenses, and make wise investments.

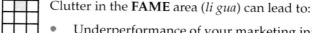 Clutter in the **FAME** area (*li gua*) can lead to:

- Underperformance of your marketing initiatives
- A reputation for being "old school" (versus "cutting edge")
- Undeserved damage to your professional reputation
- Difficulty gaining recognition for your accomplishments
- Lack of a clear future vision for your business, or the next steps to get you there

  Clearing clutter here will help you become a star in your field.

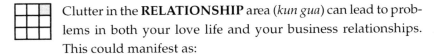 Clutter in the **RELATIONSHIP** area (*kun gua*) can lead to problems in both your love life and your business relationships. This could manifest as:

- Complaints from your spouse/romantic partner regarding your work habits or commitments
- Difficulty finding a good business partner or assistant, if you are looking for one
- Conflicts with your business partner/assistant
- Complaints from customers that you are unresponsive to their needs

Clearing clutter here will help you enjoy satisfying and mutually supportive business and personal partnerships.

 Clutter in the **CHILDREN/CREATIVITY** area (*dui gua*) can result in:

- Feelings of overwhelm
- Lack of creativity
- Problems with or complaints from your network marketing downline or from your children

Clearing clutter here will help you discard old ideas and outmoded ways of thinking, see your business from a new perspective, make better parenting decisions, and devise creative solutions to any problems you are facing.

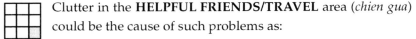 Clutter in the **HELPFUL FRIENDS/TRAVEL** area (*chien gua*) could be the cause of such problems as:

- Lackluster performance from service providers
- Mentors or advisors unavailable when you need them
- Lack of support from a network marketing upline
- Difficulty achieving any travel-related goals

Clearing clutter here will keep your lines of support strong.

Clutter in the **TAI CHI** (center) of the office will affect every aspect of your professional life, as well as having a negative impact on your health and wellbeing.

Clearing clutter here will help you handle stress more easily, take better care of yourself, and balance your work and family life more effectively.

MORE CLUTTER PROBLEM AREAS

Here are some other places where clutter may be holding you back:

* IN THE HALL

  If your home office is at the end of a hallway, clutter in that passageway will keep *chi* from getting through to your work space. Where *chi* goes, people, ideas, money, and opportunities flow as well. So if the *chi* is blocked in the hall before it even gets to your office, all aspects of your business will suffer.

* BEHIND THE OFFICE DOOR

  Doors represent access to new ideas and opportunities. A blocked door is a metaphor for blocked achievement. When your office door doesn't open all the way because there's a pile of stuff stashed behind it, you are likely to feel blocked, stymied, and frustrated. Find someplace else to stash that stuff!

* IN YOUR OFFICE CLOSET

  In feng shui, closets represent things that are secret, unknown, or unrecognized. Cluttered closets can indicate that hidden problems are impeding your progress.

  Many home offices are set up in an extra guest room, with closet space that becomes a catch-all for things that don't have a home somewhere else in the house. When your office closet is filled with clutter— especially when that stuff is unrelated to your business activities—your ability to be intuitive and insightful is stifled. Cleaning out the closet and using it for office storage only can help put you back in touch with your inner wisdom.

How Much Free Space is Enough?

As a general guideline, try to keep 20% or more of the spaces in your home office available for growth. That means at least one-fifth of your file drawers, shelves, desk drawers, etc., should be unused at all times. As new papers, books, office supplies, or inventory is brought in and new files are created, look around for outdated things that can be cleared away in order to maintain this essential "breathing room."

If this goal seems unattainable, recognize the constricting effect overfilled spaces will have on your business. If you can't get rid of significant amounts of whatever your office is full of, either invest in more storage capability (filing cabinets, bookshelves, etc.) or seriously consider moving your office into a larger room in the house.

Be aware that in a small office, adding more storage capability in the form of filing cabinets and bookcases may provide more shelf space at the expense of floor space. If your space looks and feels cramped, that's a reliable sign that your office is too small.

Clutter Comes in Many Forms

Many people admit they "need to get organized," without realizing that what they really need first is a good clutter-dump. Otherwise, all they will be doing is organizing the mess. Other people think they don't have a clutter problem because their home office is tidy and organized— but what they really have is a lot of tidy and organized clutter.

It's easy to see that untidy and disorganized things are clutter, but things that you do not use or appreciate are also clutter, no matter how neatly stored or potentially useful they may be. In a very small space, things that you do need, use, or enjoy become clutter if you don't have any place to keep them.

Anything left unfinished for long is clutter as well. Some unfinished tasks and projects take up physical space, while others create mental clutter (they may not take up much room in your office, but they're why your head feels like it's about to explode).

I like to think of clutter as "all the little stuff that gets in the way of your ability to move through your day with grace, serenity, and self-respect."

You probably need to do something about the clutter in your home office if you:

- Feel stressed or exhausted when you look around your office

- Have started to clean up many times, but feel overwhelmed and soon give up

- Have spent days or even weeks over the past few years organizing and reorganizing your filing systems, but you still can't find things when you need them

- Have trouble deciding to get rid of things

- Work in a small space; there just isn't enough room for your stuff

- Frequently spend more than five minutes finding the file or piece of paper you're looking for

- Have multiple "to be filed" folders or "miscellaneous" boxes

- Have multiples of things like scissors, tape dispensers, and calculators because that makes it easier to find one when you need it

- Keep old, worn-out, or broken office equipment or gadgets lying around and taking up space

- Haven't gotten around to returning things that belong to someone else, or that belong somewhere else in the house

- Have a closet full of stuff that "might come in handy some day"

- Live in fear that people will find out what your office really looks like most of the time

A good filing system is key to keeping paper clutter under control. If you have been unsuccessful getting your papers in order on your own, consider hiring a professional organizer who specializes in offices to work with you.

Maintain the Integrity of Your Workspace

Keeping your office free of household clutter can be a big challenge when you work at home. The bottom line is that your office is a place of work and you don't want to dilute that energy too much with non-work influences. Toys, games, clothes, and leisure-time reading don't belong in here.

Your home office should not be used as a storage area for things that don't have a home anywhere else in the house. If you only use your home office part-time, the chances of it doubling as a catch-all storage space are greater, so you will have to be especially vigilant.

Most people will find that greater attention to good organization elsewhere in the house will free up some extra storage space for things that are cluttering up your office.

COPING WITH CLUTTER IN A MULTI-PURPOSE SPACE

For those who do not enjoy the luxury of having a separate room for their home office, coping with clutter can be a double challenge. Not only are you faced with keeping your work-related clutter to a minimum, but other kinds of clutter are likely to find their way into your space as well.

The more clearly you have defined a separate space for your office within that room, the easier it will be to keep clutter under control. If your office is in a corner of the dining room or living room, for example, look for ways to make that area visually separate from the rest of the space. (See Chapters 4 & 5 for suggestions.)

Those who are minding small children while working at home may have no choice but to combine office and childcare in one space. If there's a playpen or other kiddie area in your office, do what you can to keep the child and adult areas as separate and distinct as possible. That means setting up separate office and "kid's stuff" activity and storage areas, so you can keep toys and baby things in their part of the room, and out of your work zone.

Clarity and Control

When we're busy (as most of us are, most of the time) it's tempting to postpone clutter-clearing and getting organized for some future day when we'll have time to do it right. In the meantime, all that unmanaged clutter will be having a negative impact on your mood, energy, and productivity every day.

Regaining a sense of clarity and order about your business is more easily achieved by putting your office space in order than by trying to order and control your thoughts in a disorganized space. The greater your feelings of stress and overwhelm about your professional responsibilities, the more benefits you will see from getting rid of the mess and organizing what's left.

Know your limitations, and get clutter-clearing and organizing help if you need it. The cost of a hiring a professional organizer for a few hours—or even days— will be repaid many times over in your increased productivity and enthusiasm for your work.

SHORTCUTS CAN BE COUNTER-PRODUCTIVE

Resist the temptation to deal with your clutter by buying more or larger storage containers to stash the stuff in. Organizing is a separate step that should only be done after you've purged what you don't use, want, or need.

It's fine to invest in more bookcases, storage drawers, or filing cabinets *if* they are necessary for the materials, papers, and resources you genuinely need and use for your business on a regular basis. Don't use them as an excuse for holding on to all the stuff that is holding you back.

When your office has been purged of the unnecessary and your storage areas are organized and accessible, you will discover a new clarity of mind and purpose. When you claim control of your office by turning chaos into order, you claim control over your business as well.

And perhaps the greatest benefit of all: getting rid of clutter makes it easier to keep your office clean...

ACTION STEPS

1) If you are moving into a new office space or have cleared everything out of your office, make a promise to yourself that you will not bring back in anything that you do not use or enjoy. Everything else should be tossed, sold, given away, recycled, or stored elsewhere.

   If you don't have time to sort through everything now, separate out the paper files and anything else that you need to go through and stage them where you can do the de-cluttering bit by bit over time.

2) If you are working on your office "as is" (*i.e.*, without clearing the room first), start by collecting all non-office clutter: clothes, toys, odds and ends, non-work reading material, etc. Your first goal is to get this stuff out of your office space—even if that means just moving it to the other side of the room if your office is sharing space with other family activities.

3) Go through your office (or office stuff, if you're cleared the room) and find 36 things you can throw out or give away. Toss the toss-ables and put give-aways in a box or bag. Put the donations box/bag in your car and make plans to drop it off at your local charity thrift shop within the next three days.

4) Gather together all the stuff that's lying around waiting for you to find a home for it (research materials, office supplies, CDs and DVDs, etc.). Sort and keep like things together: all the books on shelves; all the office supplies in the closet; all the computer disks in one place, and so on.

5) Over the next few weeks, every time there's some other task you really don't want to do, engage in a little productive procrastination: allow yourself to put off the thing you don't want to do for a little while, and spend 15 minutes putting your files in order or going through that box of assorted office supplies.

If you need clutter-clearing help or motivation,
point your web browser to:

www.ClutterFreeForever.com
www.Clutter-Organizing.com

Good Housekeeping is Good Feng Shui

Think of dust, dirt, and debris as microscopic clutter. It may take up less space than the big stuff, but it clogs up the energy of your office just as clutter and untidiness do.

Dust and dirt are irritants to your energy and attention as well as to your eyes and sinuses. The more time you spend in your home office the more important it is to keep up with basic housekeeping tasks. Getting rid of clutter will make this much easier—yet another reason to make time for that task now, rather than putting it off until later.

The Feng Shui of Little Things

It's a feng shui axiom that "everything is connected." From this perspective, failing to keep your home office tidy and well-maintained is a sign that you may be neglecting important housekeeping aspects of your business (such as keeping up with the bookkeeping) as well.

Anything in your office that is worn out, grubby, or doesn't work the way it should—whether a large piece of furniture or a gadget on your desk—will keep both you and your business from functioning efficiently.

When we are busy and focused on what needs to get done to earn a living, deal with business emergencies, or keep up with the never ending parade of project deadlines and family commitments, it's easy to let minor annoyances and inconveniences go uncorrected. "I really should get that fixed…," we tell ourselves, as we notice the loose doorknob for the hundredth time, "…some day." But it doesn't seem worth the time to deal with it today.

The unpleasant truth is that, no matter how much we might hope for it, "Someday" is never going to show up on our calendars as an eighth day of the week. The things we plan to get around to fixing some day often don't get done for weeks, months, or even years. And every day that they go uncorrected, these minor inconveniences and annoyances take their toll on our mood and patience while they drag down the *chi* of our space.

Things that don't function as well as they should bring the *chi* of poor performance into your work space and obstruct your progress in various ways. This means that those maintenance and caretaking tasks that are so easily put off for "Someday" really do deserve a few minutes of our time—if not now then sometime very soon, not "when I get around to it."

Here are some examples how the feng shui of little things might be affecting you:

- The door to your office should open smoothly and completely. If the office door does not open all the way because furniture or piles of stuff are in the way, you will feel blocked, stymied, and frustrated. In feng shui, a blocked door is a metaphor for blocked achievement.

- An office, closet, or cabinet door that doesn't close all the way or swings open when it should stay shut can imply that your private business is exposed to inappropriate public scrutiny.

- A loose doorknob can indicate difficulty "getting a grip" on important aspects of your business.

- A door that does not open easily (it sticks in the jamb, or the knob is hard to turn) implies that it is difficult for you to make forward progress and take advantage of opportunities that come your way. You may find that opportunities that should come to you go to your colleagues or competitors instead.

- Problems with the door to an office closet have the same meanings and effect as the main office door, with the added difficulty that these issues may be hidden from you.

- Calendars still on yesterday's or last month's page imply that you are "behind the times" in your business.

- An office or computer clock that does not keep accurate time symbolizes being out of sync with the business world.

- A wobbly leg on your desk chair or desk can imply that a "shaky foundation" is putting some aspect of your business at risk.

- Untidy equipment cords or anything that you might trip over are more than just safety hazards: they could indicate that you are in danger of "tripping over" something in business as well.

- That jumble of tangled cables and electrical cords connecting the components of your computer system can indicate "crossed wires" or conflicting demands in your business.

- Dirty windows imply that you are not "seeing things clearly" or that your judgment about something is clouded.

- Any office equipment that doesn't function as well as it should implies that something about your business isn't working as well as it should, either. Problems with a fax machine, for example, might indicate incomplete or ineffective communication or information sharing.

- Burned-out lights, fixtures that don't work, or inadequate lighting in the office will all contribute to a lack of vision and initiative in pursuing your business objectives. If you need more inspiration and insight, bring more light into the office—the brighter the better.

For any of these situations, the location of the problem within your office *ba gua* may indicate negative impact in that particular aspect of your business. The good news is that these kinds of problems are generally quick and easy to fix—once you get around to taking care of them.

In feng shui, little things really do matter. The flip side of small things potentially causing bigger problems is that making even a small repair can sometimes result in a much greater benefit.

Pay attention, as you tend to the little things in your office, to any synchronicities that might crop up in the next days (or even minutes!) such as unsolicited new business or marketing opportunities that might come your way.

ACTION STEPS

1) Go through your office (or the stuff from your office, if you've cleared it out) and set aside anything that:

   - Needs to be cleaned

   - Is old or worn out

   - Is out of date

   - Is broken

   - Doesn't work the way it should, even if it is still usable

2) Dust everything: desk, shelves, windowsills, baseboards, ceiling fan blades, computer keyboard & monitor, etc. (Microfiber clothes and Swiffer® dusters are great for this.)

3) Grab a squirt bottle of Windex® and a roll of paper towels, and clean the inside of your office window(s). If you can clean them from the outside, too, that's even better.

4) Clean any finger smudges off the office door and door frame and around the light switch.

5) Vacuum, sweep, or mop your office floor. If the floor is carpeted, clean it (or have a professional come in and steam clean it... you can have the rest of the house done, too, won't that be nice?).

   Carpets can collect a huge amount of dirt and dust, and in feng shui terms every particle of it is "yucky" *chi*.

6) Open any unopened mail lying around, even if you are 99% certain there's nothing of interest in there.

   When you don't get around to opening your mail, you are making a statement that you don't care to tend to all aspects of your business. Symbolically this can mean that important matters are left unattended to... even if they have nothing to do with the information that arrives in your mailbox.

   When you go through the mail, get in the habit of sorting out anything requiring follow-up and put it in your agenda book or an "action items" file so you'll remember to take timey action. (I know this seems obvious, but you'd be amazed how many people don't do it!)

7) Clean off your desk! A messy desk symbolizes a business that is in disarray.

   If you have a lot of unfiled papers to deal with, don't try to go through them all now or you could derail your feng shui efforts indefinitely. Focus on the big picture first. Gather papers into one file folder and leave it centered on the desk so you deal with it promptly.

8) Pick up everything that's on the floor. Things that are on the floor are symbolically devalued.

   What's in those piles? It may take some time to go through all that stuff, so don't get derailed by that now; place it all on a side table or filing cabinet, or even in a cardboard box for now.

   If these are important working papers for a current project and the only place you have to keep them accessible is on your floor, your office is not working for you. Maybe you need a bigger desk?

9) Clean up your computer:

   - Delete old/unnecessary/unread emails
   - Clean out your "temp" folder
   - Defragment your hard drive (let it run while you clean up other stuff, or do it overnight)
   - Run a "spyware" utility if you've got one
   - Evaluate whether or not your digital file management system is working for you. Perhaps it's time to set up a better one.
   - Clean up your digital desktop by deleting unused shortcuts
   - Back up your data files

10) Get in the habit of emptying the office wastebasket at the end of every workday, even if there's not much in it. This will help keep energy in the room from getting stagnant.

What's Paint Got to Do with It?

Getting rid of office clutter and giving the room a thorough cleaning will clear out a lot of the old, stale energy that many have been lurking in there. To really freshen the place up I recommend a fresh coat of paint.

Changing the wall color is one of the quickest and easiest ways to dramatically improve the appearance and impact of any space. But when it comes to a home office, many people are "all business" in their approach. "I just want it to be functional," they say, "I don't care what color the walls are, and I don't want to bother with painting."

Perhaps you feel that way, too. I'm not going to insist you paint your office—after all, it may already be a perfectly suitable color in pristine condition. But when people say they don't care about color or can't be bothered to paint the office, what that usually means is that they don't truly understand or appreciate what a fresh coat of paint or a new color on the walls will do for them:

* Literally coat the room with fresh *chi*

* Cover up all those little scuffs and dings that contribute to deteriorating energy in the room

* "Paint" the room with your intention to transform it into a successful home office

* Erase your subconscious association of the space with its old purpose (same old wall color = same old space; new wall color = new use for the room)

* Encourages you to put up new artwork in different places, rather than hanging any old thing on whatever hooks or nails are already there. (You'll learn more about choosing appropriate artwork and hanging it in the right place in Chapter 6.)

Unless your office has many doors, windows, and large built-in cabinetry, the walls probably make up a large portion of the visible area of the room. The role of the wall—in addition to holding up the ceiling, of course—is to provide a neutral (but not invisible) palette against which you will arrange the furnishings and décor of your office. This doesn't mean the wall should be a shade of white or beige; pastel to mid-range tones of many colors are also suitable.

My own office, for example, is robin's egg blue; this color suits my profession (writing is associated with the water element, represented by blue) but that's not why I chose it. I chose it because the walls in their original neutral "builder's beige" were so bland they made me feel like screaming, and this cheerful blue is both soothing and inspiring to me.

I spend most of my waking hours in this room, and if you spend more than an hour or two a day in your home office you should feel about your wall color as I do about this shade of blue: it should inspire and please you and make you happy to be in that space.

Color Energy

Wall color is one of the easiest and most effective ways to adjust the *chi* of your office to help create the working environment you desire. The right color can perk you up, soothe your frazzled nerves, help you focus, or send you into a deep lethargy and inattention.

Take a moment to look back at your answers to the questions on page 20 about how you want to experience your office:

My ideal home office is _____ , _____ , and _____ .

When I am in my perfect home office, I feel _____ and _____ .

As you think about these qualities, does any particular color come to mind? Perhaps you can associate a memory of feeling that way with the color of a particular place or of a favorite object or outfit.

Allow your intuition to speak to you, rather than trying to figure out logically what color might evoke a particular quality. If you have a "gut feeling" answer, make note of it. It could be the perfect color for your hoffice.

WHERE TO LOOK FOR INSPIRATION

If you haven't given much thought to color until now, spend some time browsing around the designer room photos at websites such as HGTV.com. Notice how few of these spaces have white walls, and how pulled-together a room with colored walls looks. Which room colors appeal to you?

Color is a Personal Choice

Our emotional reactions to color are intensely personal, and most people have strong color likes and dislikes. Quick as you can, think of one color you really like, and one you just can't stand. … I'll be surprised if that was difficult for you, or if it took more than a couple of seconds for you to come up with the answers.

There is an infinite variety of colors out there: just take a look at the sample displays in the paint department at your local hardware store for a small selection. Sometimes a different shade or tone of color can affect how we feel about it. For example, fuschia (bold and bright) is one of my favorite colors. But mauve (a dull, pinkish-gray horror) is my least favorite color of all time. Pastel pinks are inoffensive to me, but I don't get very excited about them. So when I say "pink is one of my favorite colors," I'm the only person who really understands what that means.

I mention this because I'm about to give you a list of color associations that you may find helpful in picking out a wall color for your office. Following that on page 110 is a list of colors appropriate for each area of the *ba gua*. I get asked for that information a lot and I know some of you are hoping I'll provide it.

However, just because a color is appropriate for the house *gua* in which your office is located, doesn't mean it's the right choice for you. There are other ways to suit your room décor to the *gua* it's in, as you'll discover in Chapter 6. Allow your personal preference to be your guide, and use the information here to help you assess your options.

Keep in mind that office walls should be on the softer end of the spectrum. Dark shades will make it hard to keep your energy up if you are using the office during the day, and very bright tones can be over-stimulating.

Stick with a neutral or pastel shade for the walls and bring in bolder colors in your choice of fabrics, artwork, and accessories. More color is not necessarily better: a small red accent in an ivory room is just as noticeable as a red wall.

HOW COLORS FEEL

- **White** — Clean, cold, clinical, impersonal, detached (*hint*: your office should reflect your personality, not mask it!)

- **Ivory/cream** — The clean look of white but softer and warmer

- **Grey** — Attention to detail; calm, clear focus; for some people grey is stylish and sophisticated, others find it grim or depressing

- **Pink** — Soft and feminine; relaxing

- **Lavender** — Soothing; associated with spirituality and compassion

- **Blue** — Intuition and creativity; good for communication

- **Green** — Subtly energizing; the color of nature; associated with fresh starts and steady forward progress

- **Beige** — Neutral, soothing; if you need a little more "pep" you'll want to balance it with bolder/brighter accessories and accents

- **Yellow** — Cheerful and alert; associated with sunshine and a "sunny disposition," but very bright yellow makes some people irritable

- **Orange** — Upbeat and stimulating—so much so that you may have trouble staying in the room because you'll want to get out and socialize rather than sit at your desk

- **Red** — Strong, confident, and energizing; can be overly stimulating if you are already a high-energy person and need to settle down and focus

- **Brown** — Grounding, sometimes overly so; not recommended unless you are a high-energy person; some shades can feel very warm and rich and welcoming, others feel drab and depressing

Colors and the Ba Gua

Each area of the *ba gua* is associated with a specific color or colors. If you would like to coordinate your office wall color with the *ba gua*, here are two ways to do that:

* Look up which *gua* your office occupies within your home (check the floor plan you marked up for the Action Steps on page 64)

* Look up the *gua* associations for your profession in the table on page 66, then look up the colors for that *gua* here

I've listed both the doorway method and the compass directions in the chart below, so you can follow the method you prefer:

Doorway	Compass	Best colors	Also good
Career	N	mid- to dark blues	grey with black accents
Knowledge	NE	brown or beige light blue	pink
Family	E	light green	pale blue, aqua
Wealth	SE	dark green purple	blue
Fame	S	red hot pink, orange	green
Relationships	SW	pink or beige	ivory
Creativity	W	white metallics	earth tones
Helpful Friends	N	grey metallics	earth tones

You can see from this list that not every color that's appropriate for a *gua* is necessarily a great choice for your wall color—it takes a rare personality to paint an entire room metallic silver, for example. Keep in mind that you can also evoke the *ba gua* through your choice of accent colors and accessories.

Color Selection Tips

- Artificial lighting can dramatically change the appearance of any paint color. Choose a color that looks good both at night when your light fixtures are on and by natural light during the day.

- If you plan to hang B/W photography in your office, it will look more dramatic against a color than against white walls.

- Artwork with very bright colors may "shout" too loudly against white walls. Use a mid-range color to lessen the contrast.

- Artwork in primarily neutral shades needs a subtle background, very pale pastels or off-white. Stronger color will overwhelm it.

- Stay with the lighter shades—the top one or two blocks on the paint strips you pick up at the hardware store.

  You want some life to your wall color, but you don't want it to be the focal point of the room. The walls should be an attractive backdrop for everything else in there.

- Keep in mind that any color will be much more forceful when it covers the entire wall than when you look at it on a 3" paint sample.

  Pick the color you like best, then buy the paint that's one shade lighter. Trust me on this. The lighter shade will look one shade darker when it's on an entire wall, and be perfect.

  The shade you think you like will also look much darker once it's on the whole wall, and you'll realize you should have gone with a lighter shade.

- Some paint manufacturers now offer small sample sizes, so you can try out several shades without having to buy a quart of each. Be sure to check how the paint looks at several different times of day and in various lighting conditions before making your final decision.

- Stick with an off-white trim color. Bold trim can work elsewhere, but in the office it should not stand out; it's not what you want to have your attention drawn to.

ACTION STEPS

What's your favorite color?

What colors suit your office according to its location within the *ba gua* for your entire home?

If you could wave a magic wand and change your wall color instantly—in other words, if time, effort, and expense were not factors in changing your wall color—what color would you like your office to be?

Even if you don't have the slightest intention of painting your office, keep these color choices in mind. You can use them to help select your office furnishings, feng shui remedies, and accessories in the next chapters.

4

Furnishing
Your Office
for Good
Feng Shui

*A*ppropriate furnishings for your home office, wisely arranged, can have a bigger impact than you might suspect on your productivity, inspiration, and success. In this chapter you'll learn how to select and arrange the furniture in your home office for good feng shui, even in a space that may present significant challenges.

For those who are moving into a new space, this section of the book will help you design an office layout with good feng shui. For those who are working on their existing space, this chapter will help you plan and prioritize improvements for optimal feng shui.

Furnishing your office for good feng shui involves:

* Selecting appropriate furniture

* Placing your desk in the most favorable position

* Arranging other furniture to allow energy to circulate

Before I get into the "dos and don'ts" of office furnishings from a feng shui perspective, I want to emphasize that there's little point in choosing a desk—or any other furnishing or accessory—solely according to feng shui criteria if you don't like how that looks. If you aren't happy with the appearance of your desk or other office furnishings, they will deplete your energy each time you step into the room—and that's not what good feng shui is about.

The purpose of feng shui guidelines is to provide you with additional information to help you make the most appropriate choices for you. All your feng shui decisions should be based both on your feng shui knowledge and on your personal style preferences. Furniture and accessories that appeal to you visually and stylistically will lift your energy every time you are in your work space.

Selecting Appropriate Furniture

In any office—whether in a corporate environment or within the home—the most important pieces of furniture are your desk and desk chair. Your desk is a symbolic representation of your entire business, and you chair represents your foundation and support. Here's what you need to know about them.

The Problem with Used Furniture

A second-hand desk or a table you find at a consignment store may make a fine desk from a purely functional standpoint, but in feng shui terms this is a questionable choice. The problem with used furniture is that the furniture carries with it an energetic residue of the previous user(s) experience—and we usually don't know anything about its provenance.

For example, let's say you're shopping for a desk, and find what you're looking for at a used furniture store. The desk is the size and type you had in mind, it's in good condition, and the price is right. It seems like a good deal… but is it, really?

Did the previous user of that desk sell off the office furnishings as part of a bankruptcy settlement, or did that desk come from a company where business is booming? From a feng shui perspective this is a critical difference, because this "predecessor *chi*" is considered to be a reliable indicator of what your own experience with that furniture might be.

This is why feng shui consultants are rarely used-furniture enthusiasts; unless you know who used that desk or chair before you, you are taking a risk bringing it into your home.

That doesn't mean you should stay away from *all* used furniture, however. Just do your homework if you can. You may have the opportunity to buy an antique or used piece of office furniture from someone whom you know had a happy and prosperous business life, in which case the *chi* you are bringing into your home along with the furniture is highly favorable.

Choosing Your Desk

Your desk, in feng shui terms, is a powerful symbol of your business persona. It should provide a stable foundation for the work that you do, present an image of success and prosperity, and—just like your entire office space—be "Goldilocks approved": neither too big nor too small for you or for the scale of your office. Above all, your desk should be both comfortable for you to work at and of a style that you find attractive.

Size matters. A desk that is hugely too big for you can imply that you are in some way not big enough for the job, especially if you are not a large or tall person. It also tends to encourage a greater accumulation of clutter, simply because there's more space available to push things aside rather than putting them away.

A smaller desk is not going to cure cluttering on its own, but it will impose some limits on how much you can get away with not putting away. But a desk that is too small for you will "cramp your style" and is likely to limit your performance in some way. You may find yourself feeling you've outgrown your job, when really you've outgrown your desk.

Keep the overall scale of your office in mind, too, and choose a desk that is a good proportion to the room. Your desk should be imposing enough to be the focal point of the room, but not so huge that it fills the space to the exclusion of other furniture.

A large desk in a small room limits freedom of movement and overwhelms the space.

A small desk swimming in a huge space may appear lost and not "up to the job."

Your desk should be a good fit to your work habits and for the necessary tools of your trade. For example, I am happy with a smaller desk than my husband, because I work at a notebook computer that doesn't require much desk space. I also know from past experience that the more surface area I have, the more I allow paper clutter to take over. My smaller desk forces me to keep the paper piles under control, which is always a good thing.

APPEARANCE & CONDITION

As you learned in Chapter 1, the condition and appearance of your desk matter a great deal:

- A desk that is unstable or rickety for any reason— such as when a leg joint is loose and needs to be reglued—implies that your business lacks a firm foundation or support.

- A card table or other folding table is intended for temporary use. When it has become your permanent desk, there is likely to be an element of impermanence about your work. This might manifest, for example, as smaller short-term projects from multiple clients, when what you really want or need is one big long-term contract.

  This does not mean you should never set up a temporary desk in your living room or out on the patio and work there for the afternoon, folding the table up and putting it away at the end of the day. You're expanding your horizons, taking in new vistas, and enjoying a change of perspective, and that can all be good. If you are doing this every day because you don't have a defined office space, however, it's not so wonderful, and the implications of impermanence are stronger.

  If you are using a card table or other kind of portable table as the desk in your office, be aware that you are increasing the risk that your business could "fold up" right out from under you.

- A desk that is structurally sound but battered in appearance implies a lack of attention to the public appearance of your business. This effect will be stronger if your office is in the FAME area of your home, or your desk is in the FAME area of your office.

  You wouldn't meet with potential clients while wearing shabby old clothes and with unkempt hair, and you shouldn't be doing business at a desk that is in need of a makeover.

DESK SHAPES

Straight lines and right angles suit logical, analytical, "left-brain" activities. Curving lines suit creative, intuitive, "right-brain" activities.

Keep this distinction in mind if you are shopping for a new desk, especially if you are venturing beyond the office furnishings world in search of a desk with some personality.

Here are some desk shape considerations to keep mind if you are planning to invest in new office furniture. These probably won't be the determining factor in your final desk choice; style, size, budget, and how well the desk will fit into the space available should weigh heavily in that decision as well. Consider these an "FYI" for those who are interested:

- **Round or oval**: excellent for collaborative thinking, creativity, negotiations, and counseling work; brings like minds together

- **Square**: good for logical, detail-oriented work, such as accounting; elicits open sharing of multiple points of view

- **Rectangular**: best for solo work—two people will tend to sit across from each other, which sets up an adversarial relationship

- **Corner desks** (*see also "L-shaped" desks, on the next page*): usually only suitable if you have no choice but to face the corner anyway (diagram **A**), or if your office is big enough that you can position the desk to face into the room (diagram **B**):

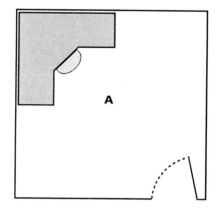 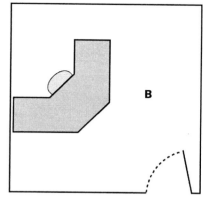

Look for a desk with a cut-off angle (diagram **B**) if you are going to face into the room; a sharp angle will create "secret arrows" of *sha chi* (you'll learn why that's not good later on in this chapter).

* **L-shaped**: Like a corner desk (see previous page), this shape encourages you to sit facing the wall. Plus, there's an incompleteness to this shape. Yes, it provides lots of room to spread out (and perhaps a little too much desk surface ready to accommodate your paper piles and clutter), but it's a shape that wants to be a square… except that there's a great big piece of the square missing:

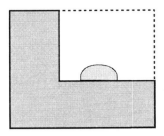

Working at a desk like this could imply that significant elements are missing from your business in some way.

If you like this kind of layout, go for a simple rectangular desk with a separate credenza or "return" to provide the extra desktop real estate you are looking for. You'll have more flexibility with how you arrange the workstation in your office, and can treat it as two separate surfaces rather than as one incomplete shape.

Is your current desk too big, too small, a bad fit for your room, or is it "just right"? What would be better that your current workstation? Whether you're shopping for a new desk now or it's on a wish list for some more prosperous day in the future, imagine what your perfect desk might be like. What does it look like, what size is it, what color? Is it sleek and modern, a comfortable country style, or elegantly ornate?

Don't be limited by what's on the showroom floor at your local office superstore. Many dining tables or even a console table might work very well as a desk for you, depending on your needs and the size of your office.

Avoid settling for a compromise: "It's not what I really wanted, but I guess it will do." Your desk is a microcosm of your entire business. Do you want your business experience to be "not what I really wanted, but I guess it will do," or do you want to be passionate and inspired and excited about your work and delighted by your results? Having a desk that you really love will help you love what you do and stay energized and happy while you are doing it.

DESK MATERIALS

Feng shui divides all things into five categories or "elements"—WATER, WOOD, FIRE, EARTH, and METAL.* Each element describes certain qualities of *chi*, and is associated with specific shapes and colors:

WATER	WOOD	FIRE	EARTH	METAL
flowing connecting communicating intuitive	integrity progress growth uplifting	intensity excitement expansiveness illumination	stability grounding supportive receptive	incisive discerning clarity focus
meandering irregular wavy	vertical stripes columns	points triangles flame shapes	flat boxy hollow	circles ovals spheres
blues black	green	reds hot orange	earth tones yellow	white grey metallics

Glass, by the way, is considered a water-type material. A good way to remember this is that glass is formed while in a molten (liquid) state and looks like frozen water when solid.

The material, shape, and color of your desk evoke the *chi* of one or more of these five elements. And the qualities associated with each of those elements will—theoretically—either resonate or be dissonant with the kind of work that you do.

Shape and color are important factors; don't assume that your wooden desk is a strong representative of WOOD *chi*. The typical rectangular wooden desk is brown and boxy, with a flat surface. These are all

* *You'll learn more about the five elements and how to use them in Chapter 6.*

EARTH *chi* qualities. The desk may be made out of wood, but that wood is no longer living; it carries very little WOOD energy compared to a lush green house plant or a live tree.

Consider the two desks shown below. Both are made of wood. Desk **A** is enclosed and boxy, and is finished with a dark mahogany stain. The primary element this desk represents is EARTH.

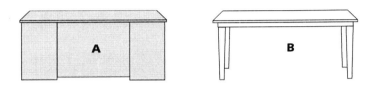

Desk **B**, also constructed of wood, has tapered legs and an open construction, and has been painted white. The flat, rectangular desktop is an EARTH shape, the legs are a WOOD shape (tall, narrow), and the white color evokes the METAL element. Because this desk carries the qualities of three different elements, the influence of each of those elements is not as strong as the EARTH *chi* of Desk **A**.

If you wished to strengthen the WOOD chi of Desk **B**, the best option would be to paint it green, rather than stripping it to the natural wood. Painting this desk RED would evoke fire, or you could paint it black or a dark blue to evoke the WATER element.

Although the influence of the five elements is just one of many factors affecting your business, you may wish to consider what flavor your desk is adding to your experience. For example, if your business has been feeling flat, FIRE *chi* can bring a needed jolt of excitement and activity to what you do. WATER energy can also help to break through periods of stagnation (think of ice melting and breaking up in the spring). WOOD *chi* brings the influence of steady upward growth. On the other hand, if things have been too chaotic lately, EARTH *chi* will have a stabilizing influence.

There are many ways to incorporate the energy of the five elements into your office; your desk is just one of them. Keep this information in mind, however, if you are shopping for a new desk or refinishing/painting an old one.

Your Desk Chair

What you sit on represents your support and the foundation of your business. If your desk chair is old, worn, wobbly, uncomfortable, or the wrong height for your desk, your business is functioning from an unstable or unsuitable foundation.

It's not important that your desk chair is business-like so much as that it is comfortable, an appropriate size, and in good condition. This is your "seat of power" so make sure it's a chair you are happy spending time in, and that it creates a visual impression that supports your success.

In feng shui terms, a good desk chair has a high, solid back for support and protection. This is especially important if you have no choice but to sit with your back to the door (see the discussion of Desk Position, beginning on page 125).

The more time you spend at your desk, the more important good ergonomics are. Swivel, tilt, and adjustable height are all nice features, but you may not need them if your chair is a good size for your height.

A chair that is too small, flimsy, grubby, or in any other way unsuitable or unappealing diminishes your professional appearance and success—even if no one but you ever sees it. If you are running your home-based business from a bargain-priced secretary's chair, plan to upgrade your chair as soon as you can, so you can be the executive of your own business.*

As always, personal preference is important, and most "executive" seating is designed to apeal to men. For my own office, I happily sacrificed all of the advantages of an executive chair for the more important (to me) joys of a chair that is a good fit for my personality and creativity. All that black leather and chrome is just not my style.

---

* Not sure what the difference is between a "task" or "executive" chair? Point your browser to one of the office superstore websites (such as **OfficeMax.com** or **Staples.com**) and look at the chair categories. If you're the boss of your business (or want to feel as though you are), sitting in chair designed for a secretary will limit your performance.

ACTION STEPS

Consider your current desk or worksurface:

- Is it an appropriate size for the work that you do?

- Is it a good scale for the room, or is it taking up too much (or too little) space?

- What condition is it in? Can it be repaired or refinished, if necessary, to improve stability and/or appearance?

What about your desk chair:

- Do you have a chair that is designated specifically for office use, or have you borrowed a chair from the dining room or kitchen?

- Is your chair comfortable for the amount of time that you spend at your desk in a typical day, or does it leave you with a sore back, tight shoulders, or a stiff neck?

- What condition is your chair in? Can it be repaired or refinished, if necessary, to improve stability and/or appearance?

Which of the five elements best represent qualities that would be supportive of your business at this time?

Water: flowing, connecting, communicating, emotional, intuitive
Wood: integrity, progress, steady upward growth,
Fire: intensity, excitement, expansiveness, action
Earth: stable, grounding, supportive, receptive
Metal: incisive, discerning, mental clarity and focus

If you will be shopping for a new desk or chair, or refinishing your existing furniture, keep the energetic qualities of the elements in mind as you make decisions about materials, shape, and color.

You'll learn more about how to incorporate the energies of the five elements into your office decor in Chapter 6.

Desk Placement

Now that you've selected your office furniture, it's time to place your desk in the best possible position within the room. Once the desk is in place, you can arrange the rest of your office furniture around it.

You'll need to have a room plan for your office available. You may be able to enlarge that section of your home floor plan to show just that one room, or you may need to draw one up (instructions, if you need them, can be found on pages 237-238 in the Appendix.) If you are drawing your room plan, take the time to measure and draw accurately; don't rely on a rough sketch.

YOUR DESK TAKES PRECEDENCE

Your desk is by far the most important piece of furniture in your office. This is true even if you use a laptop computer and frequently work somewhere else. Your desk is your command center—"Mission Control" for your business—and it should be in the best possible location within your space. Getting the desk position right (or as good as it can be if your office doesn't allow for an ideal setup) is one of the most important factors in creating good feng shui for your office.

In almost all cases, the position of the desk is most important. However, if you have another work station—such as a drafting table—at which you do a lot of your work, you should also evaluate its location using the criteria presented in this section. Which of two work stations should take precedence will depend on how much of your time is spent at each: your primary work should be conducted in the most auspicious position.

QUALITIES OF A GOOD DESK POSITION

A "feng shui correct" desk placement puts you:

* In a fortunate sector within the room, facing a fortunate direction

* In a "commanding" position within the room, facing an attractive focal point and with a solid wall behind you for support

* Far from any sources of *sha chi* (harmful energy) within the room

These three factors (lucky sector/direction; command position; avoiding *sha chi*) are all important; their order here is not an order of priority. Before we get into details, I want to point out that you probably won't be able to come up with an ideal combination of all three factors, and that's okay. The most likely scenario is that you will have to make some tradeoffs, such as giving up a fortunate direction in order to sit in a good commanding position, for example, or moving a little away from the commanding position in order to avoid *sha chi*.

If you *are* able to place your desk so you are in a commanding position, in a favorable sector of the room, facing a favorable direction and well away from any sources of *sha chi*, take a moment to appreciate how extremely fortunate you are! Most of the rest of us will be doing the best we can in less-than-perfect circumstances.

Keep in mind that feng shui is rarely about creating a perfect space and more often about making the best possible use of the space you've got. So let's get to it.

Your Fortunate Sectors and Directions

You should have identified your four lucky (and four unlucky) directions in Chapter 2. If you skipped that section or don't remember your *kua* number, take a few minutes now to read or reread the information on pages 68-70.

For your convenience, here are the tables for East and West group directions again:

LUCKY & UNLUCKY SECTORS FOR YOUR HOME OFFICE

EAST GROUP				
kua #	best	good	unlucky	worst
1	SE	S, E, N	W, NW, NE	SW
3	S	SE, N, E	SW, NE, SW	W
4	N	E, S, SE	NW, W, SW	NE
9	E	N, SE, S	NE, SW, W	NW

WEST GROUP				
kua #	best	good	unlucky	worst
2	NE	NW, W, SW	E, S, SE	N
6	W	SW, NE, NW	SE, N, E	S
7	NW	NE, SW, W	N, SE, S	E
8	SW	W, NW, NE	S, E, N	SE

Take out your office room plan, and divide it into the eight compass sectors—just like you did for the entire house earlier, but this time just for this room. (Refer to the guidelines in the Appendix if you aren't sure how to do this).

Find the sector of the room that is your **best** direction. Mark this sector on your office plan. Now find and mark your other three lucky sectors within your office..

If possible, you'll want to place your desk so you:

- Sit in a fortunate sector within the room
- Face a fortunate direction
- Have a fortunate direction behind you, if you must sit facing a wall with your back to the room

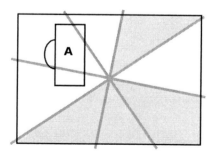 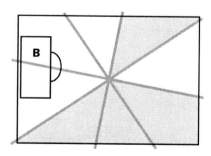

Shaded sectors/directions are "unlucky" for this person.

Desk position **A** is sitting in a fortunate sector, facing a good direction.

If your back is to the room (desk **B**), you are in a vulnerable position; it's good to have a lucky direction behind you to "back you up"

Now find your **worst** direction, and mark that sector. You'll want to avoid, if possible:

- Placing your desk in that sector of the room
- Sitting with your back to that direction (even if you are in a good sector)
- Facing that direction when you sit at your desk

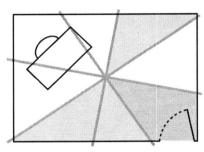

This is in the "command" position relative to the doorway, and the desk is in a fortunate sector. But the desk is facing this person's worst direction (darkest shading), which is not good. The options shown in the previous diagrams are better choices.

CHOOSING A GOOD POSITION IN A SHARED OFFICE

What do you do do if you share office space—and a desk—with a spouse or partner of the opposite group? In other words, one of you is an East group person, the other a West group person: all of your good directions are his/her bad ones, and *vice versa*.

Here are some possible options:

- Position the desk so it is *between* two sectors, one sector that's good for you, one that's good for your partner.

    Each of you, when you use the desk, can angle your chair (and computer monitor and keyboard, or notebook computer) slightly toward the direction that favors you.

    (see diagrams, next page)

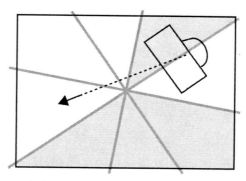

Chair angled to suit partner A (light sectors are good)

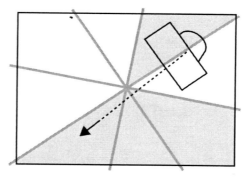

Chair angled to suit partner B (shaded sectors are good)

- If a compromise placement is not possible, and one person will be using the desk for significantly longer hours or is responsible for a larger portion of the family income, that person's directions should take priority.

- Make do with a desk that does not favor your good directions, but do what you can to face a good direction when you make important phone calls. If you use a cordless or cell phone, you might step away from your desk to make important calls from a better sector of the office.

- Trust that there's enough other good feng shui going on in the room to support your success, and decide not to worry about it.

Commanding Positions

You learned in Chapter 1 why it is important to place your desk in a "commanding position" in the room, and the relative merits and problems associated with a variety of desk positions.

Keep these points in mind as you evaluate possible desk positions in your office.

● The more of the space you can see while you are seated at your desk, the greater command you have over the space. When you are in command of your office space, you are in command of your business:

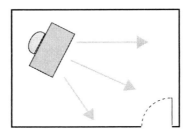

- When your back is exposed to the door, you are in danger of being "stabbed in the back" by competitors or colleagues.

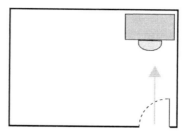

- If you can't see the door from where you sit, you run the risk of being "out of the loop" in some way.

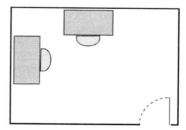

- A position directly in front of the door exposes you to excessive *chi*, which can lead to increased stress, irritability, and difficulty staying focused.

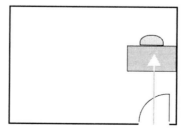

THE COMMAND POSITION IS NOT ALWAYS THE BEST CHOICE

Having just reminded you how important the command position is, now I'm going to suggest that—in certain cases—you might be better off elsewhere in the room. That's because what you see when you are seated at your desk is important.

In a small room, sitting in the command position can mean you are looking out the office door and into the hallway or a neighboring room, even if you are not directly in line with the door. Your energy goes where you eyes go, so while it's best to have a good *view* of the door from your desk, it's not so good if you see all the way *out* the door and down the hall every time you lift your up gaze from your computer monitor.

My own office, though not tiny, is small enough so that from any of the supposedly good command positions I see out the office door and down the hall to the laundry room or down the stairs to the landing. In both those positions I feel that my energy is depleted, and I am distracted by looking beyond the office to other areas of the house.

Because my office is in the front of the house, these positions also place me with my back to the street, where any noise and distractions from outside the house will be coming from. I am more comfortable—and still have a wide view of the room and a peripheral view of the doorway—in another corner of the room. Fortunately, this corner also allows me to sit in my best sector of the room, facing a good direction.

ACTION STEP

Take another look at your office floor plan.

- What options (if any) do you have for taking advantage of a Command Position?

- If more than one possible Command Position is available, do any of them also place you sitting in a fortunate sector or facing a fortunate direction?

Don't make a final decision about desk placement yet! As important as all this information is, if a position in your office exposes you to "secret arrows" or oppressive *chi*, the advantages of that location will be undermined. It's better to give up the command position than to work where your personal *chi* is under attack.

Avoiding Sha Chi

Sha chi is any form of harmful energy. In evaluating potential drawbacks to your desk positions, you'll want to watch out for these three main kinds of *sha chi*:

* Secret arrows

* Oppressive *chi*

* Electro-magnetic frequency (EMF) radiation

SECRET ARROWS

"Secret arrows" are turbulent *sha chi* created by sharp angles, points, and corners. Secret arrows attack and weaken your personal *chi*, leaving you more vulnerable to stress and irritability. They can undermine your physical health, too, if you are exposed to them for a long period of time.

Imagine for a moment that you look up from your desk and see someone standing in the corner of your office, aiming a bow and arrow at you. The bowstring is drawn back, and the archer could let go at any moment. You'd feel a little uncomfortable, wouldn't you? Your heart rate would go up, and you'd feel quite anxious and uncertain what would happen next.

Now imagine that this archer, rather than being a real person, is a small figurine, perhaps eight or nine inches tall, displayed on a shelf on the far side of your office. The artist has done a great job capturing the moment just before the arrow takes flight in great detail. But it's not real, so there's no threat to you. Right?

Not so, according to feng shui. Your conscious mind may say "it's a work of art, not a threat," but your subconscious mind disagrees. It sees an arrow pointed right at you, and art or not, on a subconscious level that feels like a very real threat.

Secret arrows are often much subtler than this example, but the bottom line is that any sharp or pointed object in your office—and any even vaguely threatening imagery—is a potential source of *sha chi*. If this seems a litte far-fetched, here's an experiment you can conduct with the assistance of a friend or family member.

EXPERIENCING SECRET ARROWS

Try this with a friend. Ask for his or her cooperation without explaining what you are trying to prove; you can say what it is about after you've finished the experiment.

1. Find a spot in your house or apartment where you can stand with your back against a flat wall, with nothing pointing at you or hanging over you. Now, find another spot in your house that has a sharp angle or point—such as a corner wall that sticks out into the room, or the sharp corner of a bookcase or countertop.

2. First, stand a few inches away from the flat wall, facing into the room.

   Hold one of your arms straight out to the side at shoulder height. Have your friend push down on your arm with steady, firm pressure, while you resist the movement. (This is not a contest of strength, moderate pressure is enough!)

3. Now move to the other spot, and stand with your back to the point or angle.

   Hold out your arm again, and have your friend try to push it down while you resist the movement. It was probably harder for you to resist the downward pressure this time. That's the effect of *sha chi* from the corner weakening your personal *chi*.

4. If your friend would like a turn, switch roles and repeat the experiment (you can start in the second position, then return to the first one).

Secret arrows are potentially harmful because—as you discovered if you performed the preceding experiment—they disrupt your energy and weaken your *chi*.

If you are exposed to secret arrows while you are working at your desk, you are likely to experience any (or many) of the following symptoms:

* Fatigue

* Depression

* Poor concentration

* Mental sluggishness

* Difficulty making decisions

* Headaches, back pain, or other aches and pains not attributable to other causes (such as poor lighting or a chair that is the wrong height for your desk)

* Irritability

* Slow recovery from illness

* Lowered resistence to colds or allergies

These symptoms are caused by the subtle physical stress of *sha chi*, and over the long term they can not only interfere with your productivity, but may also erode the functionality of your immune system and potentially compromise your health.

While the consequences of exposure to *sha chi* most often show up in physical ailments (including emotional distress and mental fogginess), the effects may show up in your business results. Secret arrows in your home office could contribute to failed business deals, falling profits, and conflicts with your clients, customers, or partners, to name just a few possibilities.

There's no way of knowing exactly how a secret arrow will hurt you, but you can be sure that some kind of damage will be done. The sharp corner of a table, the edges of a shelf, even points or angles on a lighting fixture can all cause a disruption in the smooth flow of *chi* nearby.

Common sources of secret arrows in a home office include:

● Wall corners that jut into the room. These are common in multistory apartment buildings, where the interior walls wrap around large support beams.

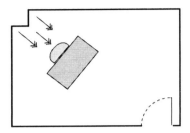

This desk position is being attacked by secret arrows
from a corner of the room

● Sharp corners of furniture, such as the corners of a credenza or bookcase. The more rounded the corners, the less of a problem they represent.

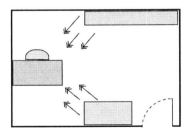

This desk position is being attacked by secret arrows
from the corners of other furniture in the room

● The slats of Levelor®-type window blinds. If the blinds are lowered and open the edge of each slat is like a knife-edge. (If the blinds are raised, or the slats are tilted closed, they are not a problem because the edges are no longer pointed at you.)

- Ceiling fans help keep us cool and reduce air-conditioning costs. However, a ceiling fan directly over your desk radiates "cutting *chi*" as it spins. Try not to place your desk or chair directly under a ceiling fan.

- Any sharp object or even imagery of a sharp or pointed object aimed in your direction.

FACTORS TO KEEP IN MIND

Some secret arrows are more harmful—or more potentially harmful—than others. How greatly they will impact you depends on these three factors:

- **Proximity:** The closer you are to the feature or object that causes the secret arrows, the more strongly they will affect you.

  A corner angle at the far side of a large room is not likely to be much of a problem. However, if you sit directly in front of it you are likely to feel the effects quite strongly.

- **Duration:** The longer you are exposed to secret arrows, the stronger their effect will be.

  If you stand near a source of secret arrows for a few minutes while sending a fax, for example, the effect will be slight. If you work for many hours a day in a position that is afflicted by secret arrows, the effects are likely to be very noticeable, and could eventually be harmful to your health and equanimity.

- **Cumulative exposure:** The more sources of *sha chi* are present in a room, the greater the total effect will be.

  The corner of a single bookcase, for example, is not likely to be a problem if you are seated far away from it. But if there are many sharp corners crowded into a space, you'll feel their stressful, distracting effect regardless of proximity or duration.

  The next time you feel uncomfortable in a space, and are not sure why, look around to see if you are being attacked by secret arrows or if there are many sources of *sha chi* in that space.

OPPRESSIVE CHI

A second form of *sha chi* you should be aware of is the oppressive *chi* resulting from overhead beams and slanted ceilings.

* **Exposed beams**

  Exposed ceiling beams create downward pressure onto the area directly beneath them.

  Chi moves across a flat ceiling smoothly and evenly. But where the ceiling is interrupted by an exposed beam, turbulence results:

  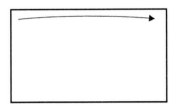 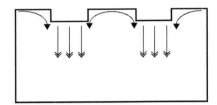

  The net effect is that anything positioned directly beneath a beam is subject to *sha chi* from overhead. Interior designers may be fond of exposed beams and extoll the character they give to a room, but feng shui professionals see them as a serious problem to be avoided if at all possible.

  A beam over your desk may make it difficult to concentrate on your work, cause frequent headaches, or you may feel weighed down with business problems and worries. The lower the ceiling, the greater the impact will be.

* **Slanted Ceilings**

  Chi flows down the slope of a slanted ceiling and puts pressure on whatever is against the lower wall.

  The height of the ceiling, the angle of slope, and the overall size of the room all affect the amount of pressure created. If you cannot stand upright on the lower side of the room without bumping your head, the situation is considered severe.

If your desk is on the low side of a room with a slanted ceiling, you will be under the pressure of oppressive *chi* while you work:

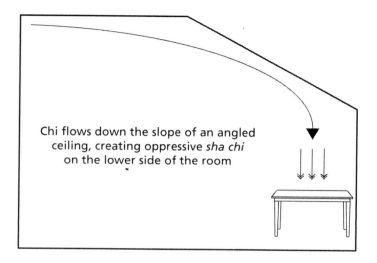

Chi flows down the slope of an angled ceiling, creating oppressive *sha chi* on the lower side of the room

In addition to the oppressive *chi* under the low side(s) of the ceiling, the angled ceiling creates unbalanced energy for the entire room. This may affect you (or your business) in a variety of ways:

* You may feel stressed-out, off-balance, irritable, moody, and out-of-sorts much of the time.

* You may experience uneven cash flow, lopsided business activity, or unusual difficulty winning new business.

* Others may perceive you as unstable or unreliable.

* Your health may suffer, or you may become depressed.

A "cathedral ceiling"—which is angled evenly on opposite sides of a high center—is less problematic because there is not as much of an energy imbalance between one side of the room and the other. However, the oppressive *chi* caused by the angled ceiling is still an issue. The closer to the center of such a room that you can place your desk, the better.

◉   **Tall furniture**

Try to avoid sitting very close to furniture that will tower over you
while you are working. For example, bookcases near your desk
that are higher than head-height when you are seated are a form of
oppressive *sha chi*. The secret arrows from the edges and corners of
the shelves may also cause pressure, headaches, and poor concentration.

Wall shelves over or very near your desk can be threatening on a
subconscious level as well. Knowing that the shelves are firmly
attached and not likely to fall does not reassure your subconscious
mind or offset the effects of this oppressive energy. Built-in bookcases are less of an issue because they are part of the wall structure,
rather than being attached to the wall.

Place your desk so it will be a comfortable distance away from any
high shelving units or other tall furniture such as an armoire or TV
cabinet.

ELECTRO-MAGNETIC FIELD (EMF) RADIATION

One of the most prevalent—and potentially dangerous—forms of *sha
chi* affecting us today is something that ancient feng shui masters never
encountered: the harmful EMF (electro-magnetic field) pollution generated by electrical appliances and wiring in our homes and offices,
and the microwave radiation of wireless communication networks.

We position our desks for optimal energy, then spend many hours
a day exposed to high levels of EMF radiation from our computers and
cell phones, and wonder why we suffer from headaches and fatigue by
the end of the day.

Recent epidemiological studies have generated a substantial body
of evidence linking EMF exposure to impaired brain function and behavioral disorders, headaches, fatigue, an increased risk of cancer, and
degenerative diseases such as Alzheimer's and Parkinson's.*

---

* For a summary of recent research in this area, visit **www.EMF-Health.com**

Research scientists now confirm that the natural electromagnetic pulses from the brain that regulate our bodily systems and manage health and well-being are significantly disrupted by the EMFs from man-made devices. Furthermore, EMF exposure can lead to defective cell metabolism, which over time can lead to a multitude of health problems. If you have ever noticed feeling drained and exhausted after a long session in front of your computer, or have had a sensation of heat or buzzing in your ear after using your cell phone, you are experiencing this for yourself.

Regardless of how perfect a desk position may appear to be in all other ways, if that position will expose you to high levels of EMF radiation, it should be avoided. Some obvious sources of EMF, such as a window air-conditioning unit, are easy to avoid. Others are not so easy to spot, including something that may be close by but on the other side of a wall, such as a fuse box or major appliance such as an air conditioner, refrigerator, hot water heater, etc. Keep in mind that a source of EMF *sha chi* may be above or below your office, or even on the exterior of the home, such as a central A/C unit or electrical junction.

Proximity and duration are important factors in EMF exposure. And although brief exposure to other forms of *sha chi* is generally not a problem, frequent brief exposure to high levels of EMF can have a cumulative effect. Given that most home offices are filled with electronic equipment such as computers, printers, and fax machines, it makes sense to limit additional exposure as much as possible.

As EMF pollution has become more widely recognized as a serious threat to our well-being, leading-edge technologies are being used to develop solutions, including:

* Plug-in devices that render background EMF less harmful

* Small "chips" to place on your computer and cell phone

* Pendants that are worn around the neck to strengthen your biofield and reduce the effects of EMF-related stress on your system.

I use these devices in my own home and office (and wear a "QLink" pendant from **EMF-health.com**) to counteract the effects of the many hours I spend each day in front of the computer.

EMF Health Resource

For more information on this topic, download the free ebook, **EMF Dangers and Solutions**, available at **EMF-Health.com**.

ACTION STEPS

Secret Arrows
Look around your office to see if any of your potential desk positions will expose you to "secret arrows" of *sha chi*.

If there is no desk position available to you that is safe from secret arrows, make note of the specific problem so you can take appropriate corrective action as specified in Chapter 5.

Oppressive Chi
Does your office have exposed beams or an angled ceiling?

Avoid—if possible—any desk position that is under an exposed beam or at the lower side of a room with an angled ceiling.

If you cannot avoid oppressive *chi* in your office, make note of the problem so you can implement any of the corrective strategies provided in Chapter 5.

EMF Exposure
What significant sources of EMF *sha chi* might your home office—or certain areas of your office, be exposed to? Be sure to examine:

- Your office itself

- What's on the other side of your office walls

- What's overhead or underneath your office.

Choose a desk position that minimizes your exposure to high electro-magnetic fields from any fixed sources in the house or in close proximity on the exterior.

Weighing Your Options

Now you are armed with the information that you need in order to weigh the pros and cons of the desk positions available to you: location of your auspicious sectors and directions; possible command positions available within your room; and any sources of *sha chi* to be avoided or remedied.

As I mentioned at the beginning of this section, there's no clear-cut priority among these different factors. Your goal is to find the best option or options available to you given the specific layout and features of your space.

It's also important to make your desk placement decision based on how you feel and what you see in different areas of your office, and not to rely entirely on the room layout assessment. Every space is unique, and you are the best judge of the specific qualities of your space.

HOW IMPORTANT IS IT TO BE "LUCKY"?

How much emphasis to give to your personal auspicious directions will depend to some extent on whether the office itself is in one of your fortunate sectors within the home.

* If the entire office is in a fortunate sector of your home, you won't need to give much emphasis to placing the desk in a fortunate sector of the office.

* If your office is in an *un*fortunate sector of the entire home, try to counteract that influence by placing the desk in a fortunate sector within the office if you can.

* If you can place your desk both within an auspicious sector of the office *and* facing an auspicious direction, that's a double dose of good fortune.

* If you can't manage both, it's better to sit in an unlucky sector of the room but facing a good direction than it is to sit in a lucky sector facing an unlucky direction.

Here's a summary of advantages and challenges to consider:

EVALUATING YOUR DESK POSITION

BEST

* You face a lucky direction when seated at your desk

* Your desk is in a lucky sector of the office

* You have a good view of the entire room, including the doorway, and have a solid wall at your back

* Neither you nor your desk are exposed to secret arrows or other forms of *sha chi*

GOOD

* You face a lucky direction when seated at your desk

* Your desk is in a lucky sector of the office, **or** your office is in a lucky sector of your home, but not both

* You can see the doorway from where you sit, but there is a window behind you

* Neither you nor your desk are exposed to secret arrows or other forms of *sha chi*

REMEDIES NEEDED

* You can see the door from where you sit, **or** you can face a lucky direction ... but not both

* Your desk is in a lucky sector of the office, **or** your office is in a lucky sector of your home ... but not both

* You are unable to avoid some exposure to *sha chi*

AVOID

* Your office and desk are both in unlucky sectors

* You face an unlucky direction

* You sit with your back to the room or (worse) with your back to the door

* You or your desk are attacked by "secret arrows" or exposed to other forms of *sha chi.*

Desk Position in a Mixed-Use Space

The more serious you are about working from home, the more critical it is to define a specific space that is your "office"—even if that office shares a room with other activities. Remember that both your office and your desk are microcosms of your business, and deserve the best possible situation. The compromises that you make in a shared space define the value that you place on the work that you do.

As with other less-than-ideal situations, the key is to use your knowledge of feng shui to find the best possible options among those available to you. If your choices are extremely limited, use what you have learned about favorable desk positions to identify the advantages and challenges of your desk position so you can choose and implement appropriate remedies as suggested in the next chapter.

OFFICE IN THE DINING ROOM

Here the main issue is how frequently the room is used for dining, and how exclusively you are able to use that space for work. Do your kids also use the table to do homework in the afternoons or evenings, or do you have the room to yourself? Are you using the table as a desk during the day, then clearing your things away for family dinner each night? Or do you have use of this room as your office most of the time, packing up to make room for special occasion meals from time to time?

One advantage to working at the dining table is that you have a number of seats to choose from: pick one that puts you in as favorable a position as possible in terms of your lucky direction, without sitting with your back to the door or where you are exposed to *sha chi*. The disadvantage, if you are vacating the area so it can be used for family dinners every night, is that you really don't have an office: you have a temporary work area.

If this is the case, where are you stashing your things when dinner time comes around? Are your work materials stashed here and there around the room, wherever there's an available nook or cranny? If a stranger were to walk into this room, would he or she see an "office" or a very untidy and cluttered dining room?

What you want to avoid is spreading a mess of "office" clutter over half (or all) the dining table during the day, then simply pushing things aside in the evening so you and your spouse have space to eat at the other end of the table at night. This kind of untidy co-mingling of work and dining is not supportive of either professional success or healthy eating. Either take over the dining room as your office and agree to eat in the kitchen, or find some way to keep your work tidy and separate.

The more temporary your working quarters, the more important it is that you have some kind of designated storage space for your things, so your "office" doesn't turn into a heap of papers stashed on an extra chair when you're not working. Take over a section of a wall-unit, one drawer in a sideboard, or a shelf or two in the bookcase in the corner of the room, so you can:

* Define a specific part of that space as your own

* Put away the files and materials you work with every day easily and quickly when you are not using them

* Retrieve your "office" conveniently when you are ready to set up shop again

OFFICE IN THE LIVING ROOM

The main problem with working in the living room is that work and recreation/relaxation are not a good mix. When these two energies are combined in one space, you may find it hard to concentrate on work when you need to, and difficult to relax and stop thinking about work when you want to.

The key to working successfully in the living room is to make a conscious choice about how much priority to give to the work function, compared to TV time (or whatever other leisure activites take place in there).

This will depend on whether the work that you do at home is your full-time employment, a part-time occupation that you would like to grow into something larger, or a sideline that is as much a hobby as a part-time profession. The more critical your home-based work is to your income, the more priority it should take in the space.

What usually happens when you work in the living room is that the desk is placed in whatever corner is available, and the couch and television set continue to dominate the room. A better solution is to divide the room into two separate areas with screens, area rugs, house plants, curtains—whatever will create physical and visual separation. Bookcases can be placed to create a half-wall, for example, and you can paint that area of the room a different color. You might consider getting a smaller sofa, or moving a side chair or two elsewhere in the house to make more room for your office.

Use your feng shui knowledge to help you decide which part of the room is best suited for use as your office. If you do a good job of dividing the room into two separate spaces, you can apply the *ba gua* just to the part of the room that is your office, and arrange that area as though it were a separate room:

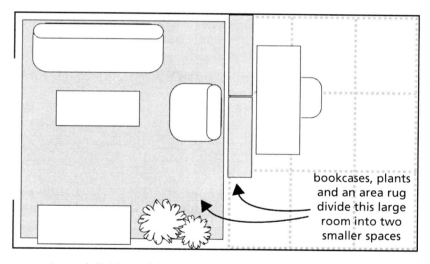

bookcases, plants and an area rug divide this large room into two smaller spaces

A good division of the space allows you to apply the *ba gua* to the office as though it were a separate room

At the very least, negotiate with your family members for uninterrupted use of the room when you need it. Arrange a schedule for when the room is your office and when it's the living room, and/or establish clear signs, such as a closed door means Mom is working and is not to be interrupted.

OFFICE IN THE BEDROOM

Working in the bedroom, like working in the living room, creates a conflict between incompatible energies. You are likely to find it difficult to concentrate and may succumb to the tempation to lie down for a quick nap a little too frequently. At night, you may find it difficult to set work aside, and your brain is likely to be working overtime while your body is trying to go to sleep.

If your bedroom is large enough, see if you can create two separate spaces (see "Office in the Living Room"): one for sleeping, one for working. If you can't erect some kind of a divider, or the desk is clearly visible when you are in bed, do what you can to hide your work at night. Close your notebook computer, and put files and papers away. If you are using a desk-top computer, drape a scarf over the monitor.

The biggest challenge for an office in the bedroom is that it's very possible you won't be able to get both your desk and your bed into favorable positions. If that's the case, the bottom line is that it's more more important to use your best options for sleeping than for working.

When sleeping, the top of your head should point in favorable direction; if the bed is also in a good sector within the room, that's even better. Your body rests and repairs itself during sleep, so it is also very important that you not sleep in an area with high EMF fields or that is exposed to other forms of *sha chi*. If you must make a trade-off, choose the less-affected location for your bed, rather than your desk.

As appealing as it might be from a space-saving point of view, I hope you will resist the temptation to build a loft bed over your work area. This creates *horrible* feng shui both for your bed and for your desk. The cramped head room above and oppressive *chi* below will severely limit your ability to do good work or get a good night's sleep. Don't do it unless you are in a converted industrial space with at least 15-foot ceilings. Even then, it should be a last resort.

You should also avoid storing any kind of work-related materials under your bed. All that mental energy underneath you will make it hard to get a good night's sleep. If you must use the area underneath your bed for storage, use it only for extra bedding and towels, or for storing off-season clothes or other soft items.

Ensuring a Good Flow of Chi

Getting your desk into the best position is the most important aspect of arranging the furniture of your home office. After that, it's a question of balancing functionality with a good flow of *chi* through the space.

In your office, an adequate circulation of *chi* means good energy for your business. Healthy *chi* circulation brings with it vitality, inspiration, opportunities, and insight; you want to make sure a good flow of *chi* is getting to your office, and can circulate within the room once it gets there.

Where *chi* does not flow, it becomes stagnant, just as water does. And where it flows too strongly it brings with it tension and aggravation. Here's what you should know:

* In rooms with good *chi* we feel relaxed, cheerful, and alert. We take an interest in others, and are more likely to feel absorbed in and inspired by our work. We can focus easily on the tasks at hand and use our time efficiently, without feeling washed out or distracted.

* In rooms with very low *chi* we feel draggy and tired, unable to summon up the energy to get much done. Our outlook can turn gloomy and discouraged, and we easily sink into apathy or depression. Even simple tasks can seem overwhelming or not worth the effort.

* In rooms with excessive *chi* we feel irritable, scattered, stressed, and argumentative. We have difficulty coping gracefully with the day-to-day challenges of life, and may be unable to get along easily with others. Even minor issues can lead to feeling fed up with projects, people, or situations, and it is often difficult to maintain the focus necessary for completing tasks and projects.

There are many ways to use décor and accessories to improve the *chi* of a space. Before looking at issues of décor—which we will do in the next chapter—your first steps should be to ensure an adequate and appropriate flow of *chi* both to and through the office.

Your Office Door is a "Mouth of Chi"

When we look at an entire building or other discrete space—such as an apartment, which is a separate space within a larger building—the front door is called the "mouth of *chi*." Just as your own mouth is the opening through which nourishment enters your body, nourishing *chi* comes into your home through the front door.

Because your home office has a function distinct from the rest of your household activities (which center around your personal/family life, rather than business), we can look at the door to your office as being a "mouth of *chi*" for your business.

CALLING ATTENTION TO YOUR SPACE

In a large home with many rooms, it's a good idea to distinguish the door to your office from the other rooms in the house, so it stands out as a separate from the rest of the house. Some ways to do this include:

* Painting the door to your office a different color from the doors of the rest of the house (choose a color appropriate for that *gua* or compass sector, according to the chart on page 110).

* Treating it as though it were an exterior door: put a knocker on the door; place a door mat or small area rug outside the door

* Hanging a sign on or beside the door to identify that this is a place of business

In a shared space, the actions you have already taken (or plan to take) to set your office area apart from the rest of the room, will serve this purpose well.

CHI FLOW TO YOUR OFFICE

Your first priority is to ensure that your office is neither starved for *chi* nor overwhelmed by an excess of it. You can get a sense of how well *chi* is flowing to your office by examining your own movements and those of your family. *Chi* goes where people go, and it moves as you move:

* Where you move freely and comfortably, *chi* does the same

- Where you move slowly and carefully, watching your step around obstacles, the flow of *chi* will be slow and difficult as well

- Where you rush around, feeling clumsy or scattered, *chi* is moving too rapidly

WALKING THE PATH OF CHI

Take a few minutes to walk slowy and consciously from the front door of your home to the door to your office. If your office is in a shared space, also include the path through that room to the part of the room that is your work space.

Pay attention to how you move, where your path is unobstructed, and where you might have to step over, sidle around, or watch your step near objects or furniture that are in your way. Imagine that you are a gently flowing stream: where do you flow smoothly, and where do you slow to a trickle or gather momentum?

Anything that slows you down as you move through your home and office is also an obstacle to *chi*. Make a note of any clutter or poorly placed furniture, and remove or reposition it as soon as you can.

If your office is at the end of a hallway, or at the far end of a large multi-purpose room, *chi* may be approaching too rapidly.

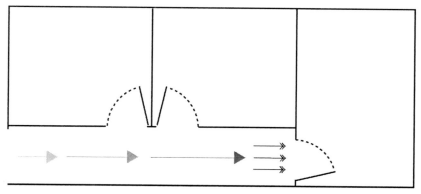

Chi accelerates down long, straight paths

Creating a gentler flow of *chi* into your space can reduce your stress level and help you get through the day with greater equanimity. (You'll learn how to adjust the flow of *chi* through your space in Chapter 5.)

Chi Flow Within Your Office

Chi comes in the main office door and circulates around the room, exiting through other doors and windows.

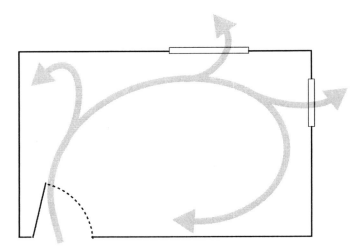

If your office door does not open all the way due to furniture or boxes in the way, you are blocking the flow of *chi*—vitality, inspiration, and opportunities—to your business. Make sure your office door opens completely and easily, and that nothing is stored behind it.

If your office windows are open and there's a steady breeze through the room, *chi* may be coming in the windows and leaving through the door. This effect is temporary, lasting only so long as the windows remain open and the breeze continues to blow. If the breeze is strong enough to blow papers off your desk, there's too much *chi* coming through: close the window!

The number and position of doors and windows in your office is the primary factor in how *chi* moves through the space:

- If *chi* flow is blocked, the energy in the office will stagnate, and so will your business; you are likely to feel that no matter how much time you spend at your desk, you just don't get much done.

- If *chi* flows too quickly through your office, it will be difficult for you to benefit from the energy and opportunities that it brings; you may feel as though you are working frantically at many different tasks without reaping much benefit from your efforts.

HOW YOUR OFFICE LAYOUT DIRECTS CHI

Here's a brief review of some typical room layouts, and how they affect *chi* flow (suggested remedies are provided in Chapter 5).

- **One door, one or two windows** (see diagram, previous page)

  This type of layout encourages *chi* to move around the space before exiting out the windows or a secondary door.

- **One door, no windows:**

  Chi comes in but there's no place for it to go except back out the way it came in. This creates creates confusion and a bottleneck at the doorway. The corners of the room are likely to feel "dead."

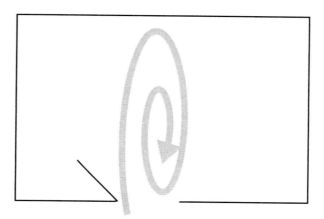

You may feel that "you don't know if you are coming or going," directionless, muddled-headed, and uninspired in this space. Good ventilation, natural light, and a pleasant view are *chi* indicators: this room has none of these important features.

- **Two aligned doors**, no (or very small) windows

  Here the *chi* comes in one door and goes straight through the room and out the other door. The *chi* flow between the two doors is too strong, but in the rest of the room *chi* is weak.

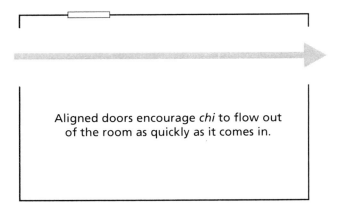

Aligned doors encourage *chi* to flow out of the room as quickly as it comes in.

  This room layout is common in city townhouses that have been converted to floor-through apartments. In a room in the middle of the apartment any windows (if there are any) are small and open onto an airshaft, providing little in the way of ventilation and natural light.

  Depending on where you are seated in this room, you may feel tense or unsettled, or be easily distracted, feeling that all the action is happening elsewhere and you ought to go check it out.

- **Too many windows** (plate glass wall, large sliding glass door, etc.)

  In a room dominated by large windows (and/or sliding glass doors), the *chi* flowing out the windows is partially balanced by *chi* coming in through the windows along with all that natural light and air.

  However, you will probably find that it is hard to keep your mind on your work, because your focus is likely to go out the window. You may spend more time daydreaming than working.

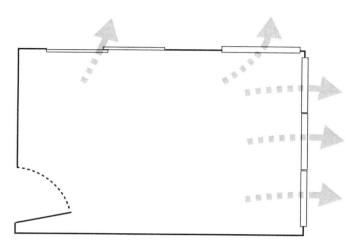

Rooms with many windows encourage
your thoughts to wander.

ARRANGING YOUR FURNITURE FOR GOOD CHI FLOW

As you decide where to place the rest of your office furniture, keep in mind how that will affect the flow of *chi*:

- Where *chi* is flowing too quickly, it can be diverted by a side table, chair, file cabinet, or bookcase.

- Where *chi* is flowing slowly, try to leave the area open and un-blocked.

- Encourage *chi* to circulate through the room by allowing access to doors and windows

- Pay attention to the corners of the room. *Chi* tends to get stuck there, and it's where clutter accumulates. Try not to fill up all the corners of a room with furniture or stuff, to help prevent stagnant energy in the corners.

  This will help to keep the *chi* in your office fresh, and by making the effort to find appropriate storage for extra things, rather than just dumping them in a convenient corner, you will help prevent clutter from piling up.

DON'T CROWD THE DESK

Proper placement of the desk relative to other furniture in the room is as important as placing the desk in an auspicious position within the room. Be sure to allow plenty of room around the desk. Crowding here will have a negative impact on your energy and the health of your business.

* You should be able to pull your desk chair out far enough to allow you to sit down and get up again easily, without bumping the chair against the wall behind you.

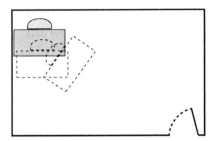

This desk is too close to the corner.
Move it further from the wall(s).

* You should be able to move around your desk comfortably. If you have to sidle sideways past other furniture in order to get to your desk, you may be restricted in your business as well.

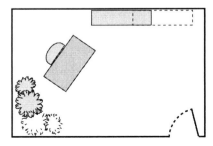

Here access to the the desk is restrictred by the bookcase and large plants; move them further away for greater ease of movement—in the office and in your business experience.

ACTION STEP

Evaluate the *chi* flow in your office:

How many doors and windows does your space have?

Is there a good distribution of door(s)/windows on at least two sides of the room, or is all the movement in and out of the room happening on one side?

When you enter the room, where does your attention go?

What happens to your energy after you have been in that room for a half-hour or longer? Do you feel:

* alert and focused (appropriate amount of *chi*)

* draggy and uninspired (too little *chi*)

* stressed, distracted, and irritable (too much *chi*)

Have you allowed adequate space around your desk for ease of movement, or do you need to adjust the position of your desk and/or other furniture?

If the *chi* in your office feels unbalanced—insufficient or too strong —there are many ways you can use furnishings, accessories, and feng shui remedies or "cures" to adjust it. You'll learn how to do this in the next chapter...

5

Remedies &
Corrections

*T*hroughout the preceding chapters you have been compiling a list of good—and not so good—features of your home office. And in the next chapter you will learn how to accessorize and decorate your office to support your ambitions and help you achieve your dreams. Before you add any feng shui "enhancements," however, you will want to plan appropriate remedies or corrections to counteract those aspects of your chosen office space and furniture arrangement that are less than ideal.

It's important to make the corrections to your space first, before adding any enhancements. Otherwise any energy problems with your space will counteract the benefit of your other measures, rendering them less effective.

This chapter provides suggested ways to make the best of the not-so-great situations you may have identified for your space. Keep in mind that these are recommendations only. You may come up with your own unique solutions that are equally effective.

For example, if a faceted crystal ball is recommended as a remedy to deflect *sha chi*, you may have another object in your office that will work equally well, such as a crystal or metallic achievement award, or a Swarovski crystal figurine.

Thinking in terms of the result you wish to achieve will help you identify potential options that may better suit your style of decor and personal taste. Don't bring objects into your space as feng shui rememdies if you do not like them, regardless of how effective they are said to be. Your own thoughts and feelings are an important ingredient in the energy of your office, so make sure your reaction to seeing the feng shui cures you put in place is a positive one.

Office Location

Very few people are fortunate enough to have a home office that does not require any adjustments, remedies, or corrections. Here are pointers for how to make the best of less-than-perfect characteristics of your office location:

OFFICE IN A MUTLI-PURPOSE ROOM

If you do not have the luxury of a separate room to use as your office, your first priority should be to make the portion of the shared space that is your work area as separate and distinct as possible. If you are creating some kind of physical partition, you do not have to block off the space from floor to ceiling; even a low divider can be effective. The key is to create visual clues that say "this part of the room is different." Some good ways to do this include:

- Paint the walls of just the office part of the space a different color than the rest of the room

- Use an area rug to define the office area; if a large rug is beyond reach of your budget, use a smaller rug under your desk.

- Use a curtain, screen, bookcases, or several large houseplants to create a division of the room into separate areas:

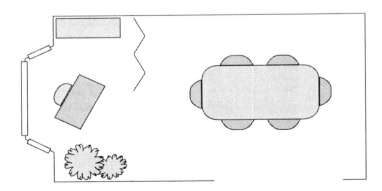

Specific discussion of issues for offices in the dining room, living room, and bedroom can be found in Chapter 4 on pages 145-148.

OFFICE IN THE CENTER OF THE HOME

The *tai chi* (center) of any space exerts a strong influence on all aspects of that space. If your office occupies this position (see page 48 for why this is not a good location), it will be essential to keep this space as open and uncluttered as possible. Be very careful not to overfill the room with furniture, and to allow for good *chi* circulation. Any clutter and untidyness in this area will affect your entire home, as well as your business activities.

The *tai chi* represents health and balance. It's a good idea to make sure that all five of the feng shui elements—WATER, WOOD, FIRE, EARTH, and METAL—are represented here in some way. (Details on working with the five elements are covered in Chapter 6.)

OFFICE AND MASTER BEDROOM IN FRONT HALF OF HOUSE

If the adults' spaces in the home are in the front of the house, with the children's areas (such as a play room, or the kids' bedrooms) in the back of the house, the children are in the commanding position within the home. This is an upset of the natural order; reclaiming a position of authority not only supports your role as parent, but will also help to prevent your children's needs and demands from interrupting your work to an unwarranted degree.

To reclaim control of your home, place a photograph of you (and your spouse/partner, if you have one) in a commanding position in the playroom or children's rooms to establish your presence. A formal portrait with parents in back and children in front is also appropriate for this purpose.

It will help as well if you make an effort to keep your office "for business only." Be vigilant about keeping family items and activities out of your space to whatever extent is possible or practical for your household. In a shared space, do what you can to keep the office area separate and clear of non-office items.

It's okay to have photos of your family in the office, so long as you take care to place them well away from a commanding position within that room, such as on the wall beside the door.

OFFICE IN THE ATTIC OR ROOM WITH A SLANTED CEILING

The most common problems with attic rooms are caused by low and slanting ceilings. Not only do these cause oppressive *sha chi* on the lower side of the ceiling (see pages 138-139), but there may also be "secret arrow" *sha chi* from angled corners and dormer windows.

Follow the guidelines in Chapter 4 for desk positioning, avoiding the lower side of the room if at all possible. That part of the space is more suitable for storage than for work activities, so put your bookcases or storage cabinets there.

Uplights under the lower side of the ceiling can help to lift the *chi* on that side of the room and counteract the oppressing *sha chi* there. House plants are also a good remedy for oppressive *chi*; they represent the WOOD element, which has uplifting *chi*. Choose tall plants (ficus, bamboo, palm), rather than spreading or trailing types such as ivy.

Depending on the wall height at the low side of the room, you may be able also to hang photographs or prints on the wall that will help to lift *chi* with vertical imagery of some kind, such as:

* A photo of a sailing regatta, showing triangular sails and tall masts that point upward

* A painting or photograph that includes one or more tall flag poles

* Nature photography of tall trees

* A picture of a garden that features a wrought iron fence with arrow-head shaped finials pointing up, etc.

Another potential issue with attic spaces is that you may feel "spaced out" up there. If you spend an inappropriate amount of time daydreaming in your attic office—or seem to putter aimlessly most of the day without getting much done—place natural crystals or an attractive geode on your desk, in your desk drawers, or in the corners of the room. These represent the EARTH element, and will to help you stay grounded and focused. Look for ways to add more EARTH-type energy to your décor, such as with earth-tone fabrics (throw pillows on your reading chair, curtains for the window), decorative ceramic pottery, or a stoneware doorstop.

OFFICE IN THE BASEMENT OR BELOW GROUND LEVEL

The excessive EARTH *chi* of an underground location may deplete your energy, and a low ceiling—common in basement spaces—will compound this effect. If you feel draggy and lethargic in your subterranean office space, it will help if you can:

* Minimize the EARTH-type aspects of your décor

* Add movement in the form of a mobile or other kinetic art

House plants will add much-needed living *chi* (use life-like silk ones if necessary), and can add movement as well: place a small fan so its breeze flutters the plant leaves.

Bright lights are important down here, although if the ceiling is low you should avoid overhead fixtures if you can. A torchère will lift the *chi* of the room and bounce bright light off the ceiling.

Windows in a basement office—if you have any at all—are probably small and placed high on the wall. If you can't see outside, bring the natural world inside in some way, such as with house plants or nature photography. Choose artwork that is expansive and has a sense of depth (landscape photography, for example, rather than close-up shots of trees or flowers), to counteract the enclosed feeling of the space.

Avoid using tall storage cabinets and large artwork in a room with a low ceiling (diagram **A**, below) as these will emphasize the lack of vertical space and make the room feel even smaller. Counter-height units and small artwork (diagram **B**) are a better choice, as they leave a good portion of wall space visible.

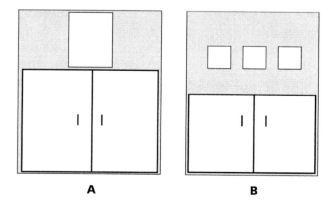

A   **B**

OFFICE IN AN UNLUCKY SECTOR FOR YOUR KUA NUMBER

Although there is no remedy for an unlucky sector, you can make the best of an inauspicious office location by placing your desk so you sit facing a fortunate direction. If that is not a good option for you for other reasons, such as exposure to *sha chi*, (see Chapter 4 for details), hang a photograph or other piece of art on the wall so that if you turn to face the focal point you are facing a fortunate direction. Turn your chair in that direction when you make important phone calls, or take your cordless or cell phone to another area of the offfice with better *chi* for your *kua* number.

Office Chi

LITTLE OR NO NATURAL LIGHT IN THE OFFICE

Replace standard light bulbs with full spectrum lighting, and bring nature inside in whatever way you can, such as with life-like silk flower arrangements, nature photography, etc. Make sure that your décor includes curving lines, such as upholstery fabric with a meandering abstract pattern or a leaf motif.

OFFICE HAS A LOW CEILING

Avoid ceiling-mounted lighting fixtures, if you can. Paint the ceiling white, and use torchères to bounce light off the ceiling and lift the *chi* of the space. Plants (real or life-like) in at least two corners of the room will help to counteract the oppressive effect of reduced headroom. (Also see the suggestions under "Office in the Basement" on the previous page.)

EXCESSIVELY YIN ENVIRONMENT

Yin spaces are peaceful, calm, and relaxing. If you work best in a private, quiet space, a *yin* environment will suit you well. However, if your energy drops after you've been in your office for a while, and you feel lethargic, bored or on the verge of a nap, the *yin* qualities of the space could be affecting your personal *chi*. Bring in some more *yang* energy to liven things up:

- Add more light or replace your light bulbs with brighter ones
- Choose brighter colors
- Replace heavy, dark drapery or upholstery with lighter, brighter fabrics
- Add some reflective surfaces, such as a faceted crystal figurine on your desk
- Add movement, such as a mobile or houseplants (place the plants near an open window, or use a fan to keep the leaves in motion)
- Play music while you are in the room. The volume can be kept low, and the music can be any style that you find pleasing and that does not distract you
- Turn on the sound effects function on your computer (unless you find it annoying)
- Bring in a small water fountain to add sound and movement to the space

EXCESSIVELY YANG ENVIRONMENT

Yang spaces are stimulating, energizing, and engaging. But if your office environment is overly *yang* you may feel overstimulated, stressed and unable to concentrate. You can reduce the *yang* influences and bring your space into greater balance by:

- Covering a hard floor (wood, laminate, linoleum, or concrete) with carpeting or a large area rug
- Minimizing bright colors and bold prints in upholstery and artwork
- Simplifying your color scheme, and reducing the contrast among colors
- Removing some objects that have shiny, reflective surfaces
- Covering bright windows with sheer curtains
- Turning off the overhead light and using task lighting instead

- Turning down volume on your phone and fax bells

- Turning off (or down) the sound effects on your computer.

- Choosing soft textures and darker colors for upholstery and accessories.

- Closing the office door or windows, to shut out external noise

- Using a "white noise" machine to mask distractions

- Decluttering: clean off your desk and all other horizontal surfaces

- Catching up on unfinished projects.

- Using closed storage cabinets rather than open shelving, to minimize the visual impact of your stuff

Office Layout

IRREGULARLY SHAPED ROOM

There are several potential drawbacks to irregularly shaped rooms. First, one or more key *guas* may be "missing" from the layout of the room.

If this is the case, you can use a mirror (the larger the better) to virtually extend the room into the "missing" portion:

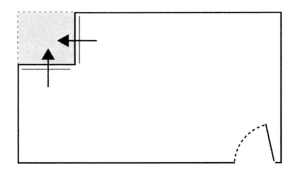

Use a mirror on one or both sides of a "missing"
corner to visually extend the room into the gap

The second problem common in irregularly shaped rooms is that corner walls that jut into the room may be a source of "secret arrow" *sha chi* (see Chapter 4 for details). Remedies for this situation include:

* Hanging a faceted crystal ball in front of the angle, to disperse or deflect the *sha chi*

* Placing a large plant or indoor water fountain in front of the angle to act as a buffer

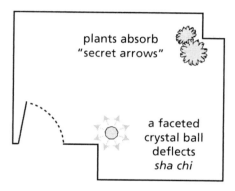

* Disguising or closing off a shallow nook with a curtain or screen, or filling that area with a bookcase or other storage unit

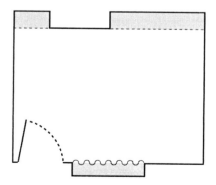

Place bookcases or storage cabinets in nooks to fill in the extra space, or close it off with a curtain or screen

THE ROOM IS TOO BIG

If the scale of your room is large for the amount of office furniture you have, don't push everything up against the walls or into corners.

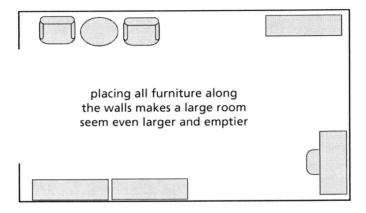

placing all furniture along
the walls makes a large room
seem even larger and emptier

Define the area around your desk with a rug, large plants, or a screen. Use floor or table lamps to highlight certain areas of the room, and make sure that focal points are emphasized (more on focal points in the next chapter) to draw attention to specific areas of the room.

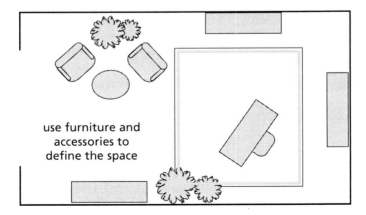

use furniture and
accessories to
define the space

Posters or other artwork should be larger in scale, or you can group smaller objects together so they don't seem out of proportion to expansive wall space.

THE ROOM IS TOO SMALL

An office that is too small for your furniture can cramp your business and keep it from growing. Look for storage elsewhere in the home that you might use for items you don't need to access daily. Most important is to keep clutter under control. Clutter will make the room look and feel smaller. Place a large mirror on a wall—preferably where it will reflect a window view—to visually open up the space.

a mirror makes a
small room seem
larger, especially
if it reflects a
window

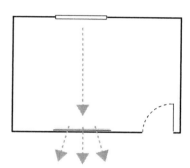

Desk Placement

As you learned in Chapter 4, choosing the best placement for your desk often involves making some kind of compromise. Here are suggestions for what to do if you have been unable to avoid a less-than-perfect desk position.

DESK HAS NO VIEW OF THE DOOR

Place a mirror to give you a reflected view of the entry to the space. You can use a mirror on the wall, or a small mirror on your desk or computer monitor:

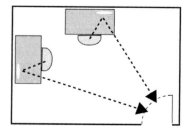

DESK IN THE PATH OF CHI COMING IN THE DOOR

This position exposes you to excessive *chi*, and can increase your stress level and lead to fatigue and irritability. Place something between you and the door, to absorb or deflect *chi*. This could be a:

* Bookcase in front of the desk

* Faceted crystal on your desk or hung from the ceiling inside the door

* Plant in front of or on your desk

* A protective figurine placed on your desk facing the door: this could be a spiritual figure, superhero, shamanic power animal, virtually anything that symbolizes protection to you

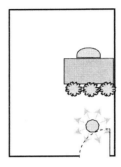

If you sit in front of the door, look for ways to deflect and interrupt *chi* before it it "attacks" your desk.

YOU SIT WITH YOUR BACK TO THE DOOR

This position presents multiple challenges, all of which should be corrected if at all possible:

* You have no view of the door (see page 171)

* You are exposed to excessive *chi* (see above)

* You are vulnerable to being "stabbed in the back" in some way

In addition to following the recommended strategies above, some measure should be taken to "watch your back." A mirror that provides a view of the door will help; even better is to place a guardian figure or image above or beside the door, facing your back.

Although this could be anything that symbolizes protection to you, my preference in this situation is for an image of a spiritual figure (such as Christ, or the Buddha, whatever is appropriate to your culture or spiritual practice)—rather than a warrior. Intend that this image will shower blessings on anyone entering the space. This fills your office with positive energy and protects you from conflict and confrontation.

YOU SIT WITH YOUR BACK TO A WINDOW

It is best to sit with a solid wall behind you for symbolic protection and support. If you sit with your back to a window, place a large natural crystal, rock, or geode on the windowsill. This will function as a virtual "mountain" behind you. An alternative would be a postcard or photograph of a mountain placed on the windowsill or on the wall above or below the window.

Be aware also of the possibility of *sha chi* from the edges of Levelor®-type mini-blinds covering the window. Sheer curtains will shield you from *sha chi* while allow light to come through.

YOU FACE AN UNLUCKY DIRECTION

There is no remedy for facing an unlucky direction; do what you can to ensure the best feng shui for your space in all other ways, and use the focal point technique described on page 166.

DESK (OR DESK CHAIR) IS EXPOSED TO "SECRET ARROWS"

If you are unable to avoid a desk position that exposes you to the *sha chi* of secret arrows implement one or more of the remedies suggested under "Irregularly Shaped Room" on pages 168-169.

YOUR DESK IS UNDER AN EXPOSED BEAM

This oppressive energy will keep your business from flourishing. If the beam also crosses your sitting position (rather than just the desk itself), you may suffer from headaches or other health problems as a result. If you can't avoid placing your desk under an exposed beam, hang two bamboo flutes on the side of the beam with red string, at an angle that implies the top of an octagon:

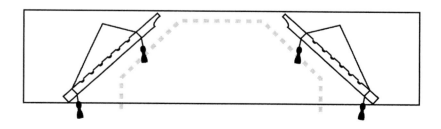

The root end of the bamboo should be at the bottom; usually this puts the mouthpiece at the top. However, if you can't tell which end of the bamboo is the root end, hang the flutes with the mouthpiece at the bottom, so air blown through the flute would travel up.

- If flutes don't appeal to you, use plants or uplights on the floor or a table beneath both ends of the beam, to lift the energy.

- Use imagery under the ends of the beam, or along the side of the beam, to symbolically lift the energy. Appropriate images include angels, birds in flight, and the like.

- Disguise the beam with fabric

- Hang a vine, garland, or string of miniature lights along the side or bottom of the beam

DESK UNDER THE LOW SIDE OF A SLANTED CEILING

While no remedy will fully counteract the effect of this oppressive *chi* , you can lessen the impact with remedies that lift *chi* on the affected side of the desk, as suggested on page 164.

EMF EXPOSURE

EMF radiation from household electronics and wireless communication networks is virtually inescapable these days. The potential health hazards are compounded if you spend many hours a day sitting in front of a computer.

A number of leading-edge companies are taking these threats very seriously, and have developed products designed to minimize the harmful effects of EMF radiation on your biofield. These include:

- Pendants that can be worn around the neck

- Small "chips" to stick on your cell phone, cordless phone, computer monitor, etc.

- Devices that plug into an electrical outlet

I use all of these devices in my home, and recommend that you do, too. For more information, visit **EMF-Health.com** and download the free ebook, *EMF Dangers and Solutions*.

Chi Flow

Chi is the vital energy that inspires and enables the success of your business. Where the flow of *chi* through your office is blocked, energy will stagnate, clutter will accumulate, and your progress and success are undermined. Here are suggestions for how to improve the *chi* flow in an office with layout challenges:

ONE DOOR, NO WINDOWS

Chi circulation is compromised by a bottleneck at the one access point. *Chi* does not flow through the office well because it has to go out the way it came in.

Make sure to keep the area around the entry clean and uncluttered, and to keep the door open as wide as possible. It's important not to position any furniture or storage in a way that further blocks *chi* flow or that prevents the door from opening fully.

Pay special attention to creating a focal point that will draw your attention as you step into the room and create the illusion that you can see beyond the walls of the room. It is a good idea also to have a second focal point with the illusion of a distant view where it is within your field of vision when you are working at your desk.

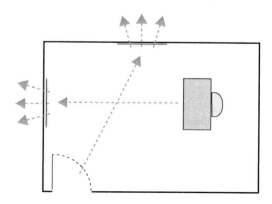

Mirrors and realistic landscapes with a distant
horizon can act as virtual windows

Keep in mind that *chi* goes where you attention goes. Anything that creates the illusion of being able to see through or beyond the walls will assist with *chi* circulation and make the space appear less confining. Some good options include:

- A mirror that creates the impression of a larger space and allows your eye to see "through" the wall into the virtual space of the reflection.

- A virtual window created by a large poster or photograph of an outdoor scene with a view of a distant horizon. The more closely this duplicates a realistic window view, the better.

- A painting or print of an interior that includes a prominent view through a window into the distance.

TWO ALIGNED DOORS

Compare the diagrams, below. In rooms **A** and **B**, *chi* flows in the main door and circulates through the room. In room **C**, the doors are directly in line with each other; *chi* rushes through the space and out again very quickly. This causes excessive *chi* along that path, and often results in depleted *chi* in other areas of the room:

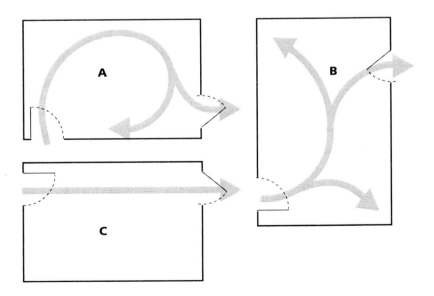

Your goal is to slow down and redirect the flow of *chi* so it can circulate more fully through the room. Some ways to do this are to:

- Use a screen, curtain, or large houseplants to partially close off the second doorway (without blocking it completely).

- Hang a large mirror on a side wall to create a virtual opening in that wall and divert *chi* over to that side of the room.

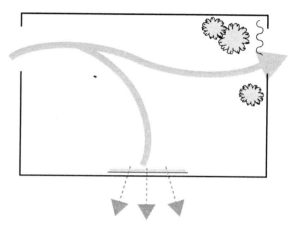

- Hang a faceted crystal ball (40mm diameter is a good size) midway between the two doorways to divert the *chi* and encourage it to circulate more evenly through the room

- Arrange furniture to divert *chi*, without blocking it.

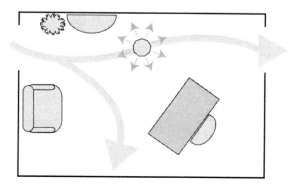

OFFICE HAS TOO MANY WINDOWS

In a room that is dominated by large windows, both *chi* and your focus and attention will be pulled out of the room. (See page 154). Curtains or shades help bring the window-to-wall ratio into better balance. Sheers minize the distraction of the exterior view while allowing natural light into the room. Be alert to how you are functioning, and if you are distracted and restless, try closing the blinds or curtains for a while so you can get to work.

A faceted crystal ball hung on the inside of each window will help to keep *chi* in the room. (If your windows are sunny, these will cast multiple rainbow refractions around the walls of your room; whether that's a plus or a reason to avoid this remedy is a personal decision.)

Bookcases below the window will help to hold *chi* in the room. Display objects on top of the shelves or on windowsills to catch your eye before attention and energy go out through the glass. Curios of all kinds can be appropriate here, so long as they are not so appealing that you get up to play with them instead of getting your work done.

A row of three, six, or nine potted plants—however many you have space for—are an especially good remedy because they bring beauty and living *chi* into your work space.

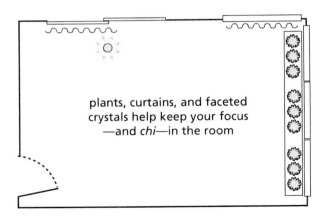

plants, curtains, and faceted
crystals help keep your focus
—and *chi*—in the room

Three-dimensional artwork that keeps your focus within the room is a better choice for this type of space than are mirrors or landscapes with a distant horizon.

ACTION STEPS

Review your notes from the previous chapters and, for each feng shui challenge you have identified for your office, note your options for rememdies or corrections based on the suggestions provided in this chapter.

Look around to explore what items you may already have available that could be used as feng shui remedies. For example:

* Artwork

* Photographs

* Mirrors

* House plants (real or "life-like")

* Side-tables

* Area rugs
etc.

What items will you need to purchase (faceted crystals, a large mirror, etc.)?

As eager as you may be to get started putting these remedies in place, I suggest that you hold off on shopping for new items until you have read the next chapter. There's a key aspect of feng shui that we haven't fully explored yet—the interactions among the five elements—which may affect decisions about the colors, shapes, and materials you choose for your "cures."

6

Elements of
Success

*T*hroughout the previous chapters you've laid the foundation of good feng shui for your office. You have:

* Analyzed the pros and cons of your office location

* Cleared out the clutter

* Placed your desk in the most advantageous position available

* Arranged other furniture to allow a good flow of *chi* through the room

* Made a list of potential remedies to correct the specific challenges presented by your space

Now we are at the final step for optimizing the feng shui of your home office: selecting and placing symbolic artwork and objects to support the areas of the room that most directly affect the achievement of your objectives.

This phase is what many people think feng shui is all about, but really it is the final stage in the process of analyzing, correcting, and optimizing your space. If you place feng shui accessories and enhancements without first identifying and correcting the challenges of your space—including removing clutter, and ensuring a good flow of *chi*—those accessories will have to work harder to deliver benefits to you.

You have already been introduced to the two main tools you'll be using in this chapter: the *ba gua* energy map and the five feng shui elements. In this chapter we'll take a closer look at how they can work for you to help you achieve your goals.

Defining Your Aspirations

If you've read any of my other *Fast Feng Shui* books, you are familiar with the idea of "power spots" as the areas of a space that the *ba gua* defines as most directly influencing those aspects of your life experience that you'd most like to improve. In this chapter we examine the *ba gua* of your office to decide which areas deserve special consideration and what accessories will best enhance those power spots.

For example, if achieving financial independence—or just getting your bills paid on time for a change—is your top priority, then *hsun gua*, the WEALTH area of your office, will be your #1 power spot. If you are doing okay financially, but desire greater recognition for yourself or your company, then *li gua*, the FAME area, is your top power spot.

While I do recommend giving emphasis to a very limited number of top priority areas within the office, it's helpful to begin by exploring every area of the *ba gua* to clarify what the qualities of that area can contribute to your business. You can then review all of these aspects to decide where you will put special attention at this time. Keep in mind that it is normal and appropriate for your priorities—and power spots— to change over time.

What Do You Want to Experience?

An "aspiration" is something that you hope to achieve, obtain, or experience as a result of your actions. The various areas of the *ba gua* are sometimes referred to as the "life aspirations."

Let's take a look at the *ba gua* now as a model of the aspirations (goals, intentions, wishes, dreams) you have for your business. As you work through this section, do not be concerned yet with figuring out where each area of the *ba gua* is within your home office—we'll get to that next.

Since by "office" we generally mean the place where we do our work, we'll start with *kan gua*—the CAREER area, at the bottom center of the *ba gua*—and work our way clockwise around the other sectors:

 CAREER

What are your career goals? Think of at least one thing you'd like to accomplish within the next six months. This can be a financially *measured* goal—e.g., "to be the top-earning associate by the end of the year"—but should not be purely financial. "Earn $5000 in commissions in one month," for example, is a *hsun gua* goal, even though the money will come to you through your career.

Perhaps your career goals are not so well-defined yet. Perhaps you simply want to work at home full time, or to figure out what you really want to do so you can pursue that instead of your day job, or to join a good network marketing company.

That's okay. Write it down.

On a deeper level *kan gua* is about how you pursue your purpose in life. Many people spend their entire lives working for money in whatever job they can get. Others find success and some satisfaction in a career that's a good match for their skills and abilities, even if it doesn't make their heart sing. Those who truly love what they do are the lucky ones, and a very fortunate few (I am happy to count myself among them) would continue to do what they do even if they didn't earn a penny for doing it.

Sometimes the best career for us at one stage in life leads to something that suits us even better at a later stage. If you do what you do only for the money, or if you no longer derive much satisfaction from your work, include finding a more personally fulfilling path as one of your career goals.

What are your *kan gua* issues at this time?

_____

_____

_____

_____

_____

_____

KNOWLEDGE

Ken gua is the area related to all kinds of knowledge-gathering and learning, including personal growth work (self-understanding) and spiritual practice (metaphysical awareness). Take a few minutes now to think about what this area of the *ba gua* might represent in the context of your home office and/or your work.

What new knowledge or skills would help you to close more sales, expand your client base, broaden your scope of services, improve your marketing, make better business decisions, become recognized as an expert in your field, be a better mentor and trainer for your downline…? Achieving a higher level of success is going to require doing something different—or doing the same thing in a different way—from what you are doing now. What might that be?

Write down at least three areas where additional knowledge or skills development will help you achieve your professional goals:

_____

_____

_____

_____

_____

_____

FAMILY & COMMUNITY

Jen gua is the sector of the *ba gua* that has to do with family in both its traditional and broader meanings. Here we focus on such issues as achieving a balance between work commitments, community involvement and family life.

In addition to the usual challanges of finding enough time for all of these important areas, those who work at home often discover that maintaining appropriate boundaries among work, family, and community becomes more difficult as well. (Your neighbors, for example, may expect that it's no big deal for you to accept their UPS packages while they're at work—after all, you're home during the day—without realizing how big an interruption and distraction these small favors can be.)

Jen gua is an important area if you are part of a network marketing business, because your upline and downline are like the generations in a family. For single people, this area covers the close friends who form your virtual family. What *jen kua* issues are you coping with?

_____

_____

_____

_____

_____

_____

WEALTH

So, you want to earn $100,000—or $1 million—this year? That's a *hsun gua* ambition. So are "to be debt-free by the end of the year" and "to increase my monthly income by 50%."

What are your specific financial ambitions?

_____

_____

_____

_____

_____

_____

Although *hsun gua* is most often referred to as the WEALTH area, a more accurate name for this sector of the *ba gua* is "fortunate blessings." Remember that feng shui is not just about helping you be more successful professionally; it is also about achieving that success while maintaining an appropriate life-work balance.

Non-financial "fortunate blessings"—such as your spouse, children, and friends, your good health, more time to give back to your communiy or just relax in a hammock—can be whatever you value most at this point in your like.

What are three important things that you would like to honor and enjoy while you pursue financial success?

_____

_____

_____

FAME & REPUTATION

This area has to do with your professional reputation—whether good or bad. It covers such issues as: what you are recognized for achieving; how others perceive your skills and abilities; and public perception of your company's products and services. Feng shui problems here can show up in many ways, such as:

* Lack of recognition for your achievements

* Negative publicity, especially if undeserved

* Inability to close sales because prospects lack confidence in you

* Difficulty defining next steps and a forward direction for a project or for your business

Li gua also has to do with your future vision and direction. *Li gua*-type aspirations include achieving greater visibility in your market, earning awards and recognition of any kind, and enjoying great "word of mouth" reputation with your customers.

How would you like to see your fame or reputation improve?

_____

_____

_____

_____

_____

_____

RELATIONSHIPS

In your personal life, *kun gua* governs your marriage or romantic partnerships. In your home office, this sector of the *ba gua* is about your business relationships, especially formal partnerships and the relationships you build with important clients and vendors.

Any situation that involves attracting, creating, building, strengthening, managing, severing, or restructuring a business relationship is a *kun gua* issue.

What *kun gua* concerns have been on your mind lately: Do you need to hire or fire an assistant? Follow up with a past customer to regain his or her business? Figure out how best to handle a conflict with your partner?

List your *kun gua* issues here:

_____

_____

_____

_____

_____

_____

 CREATIVITY & CHILDREN

Dui gua is a key area for writers, artists, designers, inventors, and work-at-home-Moms, but it also governs creative aspects of any profession. Financial planners, for example, may benefit from creative legal ways to protect and maximize their clients' assets. Real estate investors look for innovative ways to structure a deal, and internet marketers are always alert for fresh ways to reach a market.

Dui gua is also an important area in network marketing, because your downline can be seen as your "children." In other businesses, the "children" represented by *dui gua* are your employees. If you have made (or are hoping to make) the transition to home-based work so you can spend more time with your children, that's a *dui gua* issue, too.

How is *dui gua* reflected in your work situation?

_____

_____

_____

_____

_____

_____

HELPFUL FRIENDS & TRAVEL

Chien gua is the area of "helpful friends" and anything travel-related. All of the people who provide specific services to you—such as your lawyer, stockbroker, accountant, chiropractor, nutritionist, or baby sitter—are represented here, as are mentors and benefactors of any kind. If you would like to find a compatible group of people to start a Mastermind Group, for example, that's a *chien gua* goal.

In network marketing, *chien gua* represents your upline: those who sponsor and mentor you. It's important to keep this area strong so your upline will provide the guidance, support, and training that will drive your own success in the business.

Specific travel goals are *chien gua* issues as well, so if you are hoping to attend the Gold Circle Summit or take your spouse to Paris for your anniversary, include that in your list of *chien gua* aspirations here:

_____

_____

_____

_____

_____

_____

HEALTH & BALANCE

The center—*tai chi*—functions like the hub of a wheel, providing a common connecting point for all the other *guas*. The condition of the *tai chi* is said to affect all of the other *guas* as well. The *tai chi* is the area that most directly governs your health and your ability to balance work, self, and family. Anything that helps you to release stress and avoid burnout—such as working out, your meditation or yoga practice, or a weekly date night with your spouse—is governed by the *tai chi*.

For those who work at home full time, maintaining an appropriate balance between work and family can be a big challenge. It's hard to leave work at the office when the office is just a few feet away.

What areas of your life tend to slip out of balance when you work at home? What intentions do you have for correcting those imbalances?

_____

_____

_____

_____

_____

_____

ACTION STEP

SETTING PRIORITIES

Review the goals and issues that you noted for each *gua* on the preceding pages. Of all of the aspirations that you identified, which one is your #1 goal for the immediate future? What is the one thing above all others that you most want to achieve or experience in the next 3-5 years? Looking further ahead, what is your vision of the ultimate success for you and your business?

It's normal and appropriate for goals and priorities to change over time, so be sure to make your selection based on what's most important to you right now, not on what was most important to you last year, or what you think might be an issue six months from now. And don't limit your decision to what you think is realistic. Feng shui is about expanding your possibilities, so reach for what you really want, and don't settle just for what you think is reasonable or practical.

My top priority short-term goal (next 6-12 months) is:

The *gua* most directly related to my short-term goal is:

My main long-term goal (next 3-5 years) is :

The gua most directly related to my long-term goal is:

My vision of ultimate success is:

The gua most directly related to my ultimate success goal is:

You now have a list of between one and three top-priority *guas* for your home office (it's okay to have the same *gua* listed for two or even all three objectives). Let's find where those areas are in your work space.

Finding Your Office "Power Spots"

With a clean copy of the floor plan for your home office in front of you, turn the page so the main entry is at the bottom of the page. (If there is more than one door or entry to your office, follow the guidelines on page 257 in the Appendix to decide which way to turn your page)

Now divide your space into a equal nine-area grid. If your room is neatly rectangular in shape, this is easy to do: just measure the length and width of the room on your floor plan and divide that into thirds

Not all rooms are tidy rectangles, however, so you might need to evaluate whether certain parts of the room are extensions (good) or "missing" areas (not so good) for the room.

Even very small anomalies to the outline of your office can have a significant impact, so if there are small bites out of the shape of your space, or parts that stick out from the basic shape of the room, you'll want to take a close look at them.

If necessary, follow the guidelines in the Appendix to evaluate any irregularities in your space and determine exactly how to place the *ba gua* for your room.

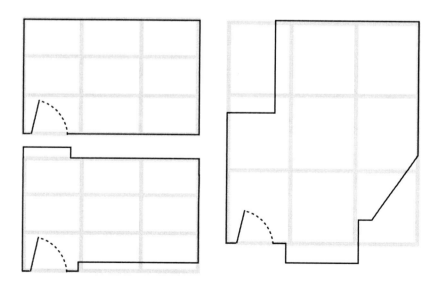

ACTION STEP

If you have not yet done so, mark the *ba gua* grid on your office floor plan with a colored pen or pencil, using the **doorway method**. Label each *gua*. With the door at the bottom of the page, "Career" should be in the center of the side of the room that's closest to you, with "Fame" in the center of the far side of the room, with the other guas arranged around them like this:

WEALTH	FAME	RELATIONSHIPS
FAMILY / COMMUNITY	HEALTH / BALANCE	CREATIVITY / CHILDREN
KNOWLEDGE	CAREER	HELPFUL FRIENDS / TRAVEL

* Which *gua* or *guas* did you identify as your top priorities?

* Where are those *guas* in your office? Highlight those sections of the grid in some way on your floor plan. These are the **power spots** within your office.

* If you have any **extensions** or **missing areas** in your office, what *guas* are they in?

* Are any extensions or missing areas in the *guas* you've identified as your top priorities?

  An extention in a priority *gua* provides an excellent "power spot" for the enhancements you'll learn about a little later on in this chapter.

  A missing area in a priority *gua* means that area is weakened, and you'll want to look for ways to strengthen it as you plan your enhancements.

The Five Elements and the Ba Gua

Those of you with previous experience with feng shui know that each area of the *ba gua* is associated with one of the five feng shui elements. There are three EARTH *guas* (including the *tai chi*), two WOOD and two METAL *guas*, and one *gua* each for WATER and FIRE. The element of each *gua* determines the color or colors associated with it.

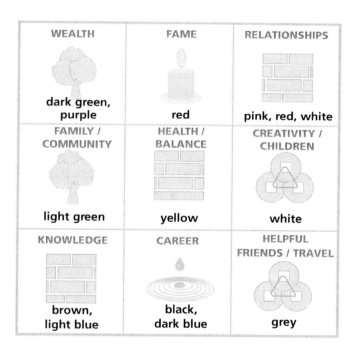

WEALTH	FAME	RELATIONSHIPS
dark green, purple	red	pink, red, white
FAMILY / COMMUNITY	HEALTH / BALANCE	CREATIVITY / CHILDREN
light green	yellow	white
KNOWLEDGE	CAREER	HELPFUL FRIENDS / TRAVEL
brown, light blue	black, dark blue	grey

The colors for *hsun gua* are green for wood and purple because it is symbolic of great success and WEALTH. *Jen gua* (FAMILY) is associated with lighter shades of green. *Kun gua*, the RELATIONSHIP area, is red, pink, and white, because it is located between *li gua* (FAME; red) and *dui gua* (CREATIVITY; white), and because pink is the color of romance. *Chien gua* (HELPFUL FRIENDS) is grey, because it is located between the pure white *dui gua* and the black of *kan gua* (CAREER). Browns and other EARTH tones are appropriate for *ken gua* (KNOWLEDGE) and blue can be used here as well.

This information will be helpful as you plan what feng shui symbols and accessories to place where in your office. For example, you can see that FIRE-type objects (lights, candles, electronics, and the color red) are well-placed in the FAME area, and that WOOD-type objects (plants and images of trees, and anything green) are appropriate in the WEALTH area, etc.

Each element is naturally strong in some *guas* and weak in others, information that you can use to fine-tune your feng shui adjustments.

How the Elements Interact

There's a drawback to the diagram on the previous page. The problem is that it shows each element isolated from the other in a tidy box: WEALTH = WOOD, etc. This implies that all you have to do to "enhance" the WEALTH area, for example, is add some WOOD-type energy to that area of your office. In reality, it's not quite that simple, and this is where many feng shui newbies go astray.

The key to using the elements effectively in your space is to understand that they interact with each other in specific ways, as described on the following pages. You can use this information to adjust the *chi* of your office power spots, by selecting furnishings, accessories, and feng shui remedies of appropriate colors, shapes, or materials:

WATER	WOOD	FIRE	EARTH	METAL
fountains	plants	candles	stones	metallic
aquariums	flowers	electronics	crystals	objects
water imagery	trees	fire imagery	ceramics	& coins
	wood imagery		dry landscapes	
meandering	vertical	points	flat	circles
irregular	stripes	triangles	boxy	ovals
wavy	columns	flame shapes	hollow	spheres
blues	green	reds	earth tones	white
black		hot orange	yellow	grey
				metallics

THE CREATIVE CYCLE

Each of the five elements is nourished, strengthened, and supported by one of the other elements. This forms a sequence called the Creative (or Productive) Cycle, as shown in the diagram below. Use the Creative Cycle when you want to *increase* the effect of an element in a particular space. Here's how it works:

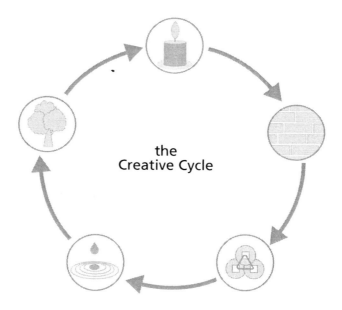

the
Creative Cycle

- WATER nourishes WOOD (without water, wood will die)

- WOOD feeds FIRE (without fuel, fire cannot burn)

- FIRE creates EARTH (as the fire burns, it produces a pile of ashes; think of a volcano creating a mountain)

- EARTH produces METAL (metal is extracted from the earth)

- METAL produces WATER (think of moisture condensing on a cold can of soda on a hot day)

THE REDUCING CYCLE

As each element nourishes the next in the Creative Cycle, its own energy is reduced by the effort. For example, you can counteract the strong WATER energy in a bathroom by adding WOOD energy to the space (green towels or plants, for example). This gives the WATER something to do (feeding WOOD, which absorbs it), reduces its strength, and helps bring things back into balance. Here's how the Reducing Cycle works:

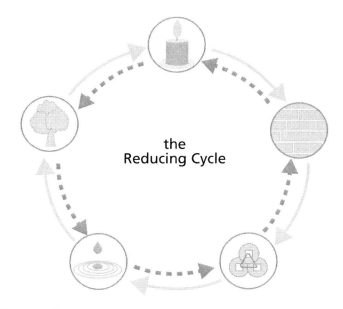

the
Reducing Cycle

* WATER reduces METAL
* METAL reduces EARTH
* EARTH reduces FIRE
* FIRE reduces WOOD
* WOOD reduces WATER

Use the Reducing Cycle when you want a gentle way to bring a situation into better balance. It's easy to remember the Reducing Cycle if you know the Creative Cycle; just keep in mind that when one element nourishes another one, its own energy is reduced by the effort.

THE CONTROLLING CYCLE

When one element is very strong, you may need something stronger than the Reducing effect to bring it back into balance. This is where the Controlling Cycle comes in handy. The Controlling Cycle works like this:

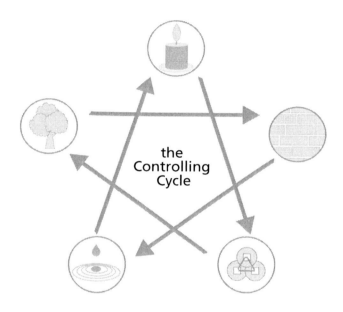

- WATER puts out FIRE

- FIRE melts METAL

- METAL chops WOOD

- WOOD breaks up EARTH (think of new grass pushing up through the soils, or of tree roots reaching down into the earth)

- EARTH dams or muddies WATER

Make sure the controlling element is strong enough to do the job. If you try to put out a bonfire with a tea-cup full of water, the water will evaporate without having much effect. Keep in mind that:

* Too much WATER can wash EARTH away

* Too much EARTH can bury WOOD

* Too much WOOD can take the edge off METAL

* Too much METAL can exhaust FIRE

* Too much FIRE evaporates WATER

Putting the Elements to Work

The key to working with the elements is to focus on which effect you want to have in a specific space or situation.

If you want to increase the strength of an element, add the two elements that come *before* it in the Creative Cycle. For example, to increase FIRE energy in your FAME area, add WATER and WOOD objects, imagery, or colors to the space. The WATER will feed the WOOD, which will enhance FIRE. You don't have to worry about the WATER reducing FIRE, because its energy is being diverted to create WOOD:

WATER and WOOD feeding FIRE

You can decrease an element's strength by adding the Controlling element, or by adding the element that it creates (the Reducing Cycle):

EARTH and METAL reducing FIRE

ADJUSTING THE CHI OF YOUR SPACE

Now that you are familiar with the five element cycles, you can see that it matters which elements are influencing each area of your office. For example, the wall color you have chosen for your office will suit some *guas* better than others. If there's a conflict between that color and any of your power spots, you can introduce additional elements—materials, shapes, or colors—to create a more harmonious interaction in that area.

Let's say you've painted your office pale yellow. This is an EARTH color, so it is "at home" in the *tai chi* (center) and in the RELATIONSHIPS and KNOWLEDGE areas of the room. In the Creative Cycle of the elements, we see that EARTH produces METAL, so this color is supportive of the CREATIVITY and HELPFUL FRIENDS areas as well. But how does it affect the other areas of the room?

Looking at the diagrams on pages 198 and 199, you see that EARTH controls (blocks) WATER, depletes FIRE, and weakens WOOD. That means your lovely yellow walls are not a good match for the CAREER, FAMILY, WEALTH, or FAME areas.

WEALTH	FAME	RELATIONSHIPS
WOOD controls EARTH	EARTH depletes FIRE	EARTH *gua*
FAMILY / COMMUNITY	**HEALTH / BALANCE**	**CREATIVITY / CHILDREN**
WOOD controls EARTH	EARTH *gua*	EARTH creates METAL
KNOWLEDGE	**CAREER**	**HELPFUL FRIENDS / TRAVEL**
EARTH *gua*	EARTH controls WATER	EARTH creates METAL

☐ yellow wall color matches or supports the *gua*   ☐ yellow wall color weakens or controls the *gua*

This does not mean you made the wrong color choice! You can adjust the energy of the negatively affected *guas* by adding something to each area that either represents the element or elements that *produce* a Creative relationship between EARTH and that area of the *ba gua*, or that strengthens the element of that *gua* to keep it strong in spite of the presence of the EARTH color in that area.

Here's how that plays out for our example:

- The CAREER area is associated with WATER. Adding METAL-type colors, shapes, or objects to this area—along with any WATER-type objects or imagery appropriate to this *gua*—will weaken the EARTH *chi* of the walls and strengthen the WATER *chi* of that *gua*.

- The FAMILY and Wealth areas are associated with WOOD. Adding WATER here will reduce EARTH and support any WOOD-type enhancements you might wish to use in this area.

- The FAME area is associated with FIRE. Here you can add WOOD energy to break up the EARTH *chi* and provide fuel for the FAME *gua*.

WEALTH add WATER	FAME add WOOD	RELATIONSHIPS
FAMILY / COMMUNITY add WATER	HEALTH / BALANCE	CREATIVITY / CHILDREN
KNOWLEDGE	CAREER add METAL and WATER	HELPFUL FRIENDS / TRAVEL

☐ yellow wall color matches or supports the *gua*   ▨ yellow wall color weakens or controls the *gua*

ACTION STEP

Which element is associated with each of your priority *guas*? Note the element for each of those "power spots" on your floor plan.

- What is the **supporting** element for that *gua* (Creative Cycle)?

- Which element **controls** it (Controlling Cycle)?

- Which elements **deplete or weaken** that *gua* (Reducing Cycle)?

Take a look at the objects, colors, and shapes currently present in each of your office "power spot" *guas*.

- What elements are represented there now? (refer to the chart on page 196)

- Are these elements helpful or harmful to the energy of that *gua*?

- Are there any items you can remove to another area of the office, to lessen the effect of that element?

- What elements (materials, colors, shapes) would it be helpful to *add* to this part of your office?

This does not mean you need to manage everything in your office according to the elements. It's not necessary, for example, to remove every possible representation of the EARTH element from your FAME *gua*; the world is comprised of all five of the elements, and it's okay for them to be mixed together in your space as well.

Do pay attention to which elements are most and least helpful to your power spot *guas*, and keep this info in mind as you choose accessories and remedies for that space. A plant is a better remedy than a crystal, for example, if you need to protect yourself from *sha chi* in the WEALTH area, because the plant represents the WOOD element and is appropriate for that *gua*.

The Problem with Plastic

Plastic is infinitely maleable, and can represent of any of the element shapes or colors. However. I don't recommend plastic as a feng shui accessory or remedy if there are any other options available to you. Plastic is literally artificial; it has no natural vitality whatsoever. Too many plastic surfaces in an environment create a feeling of "dead" *chi.*

My personal theory about why plastic is so lifeless is that it doesn't represent any of the five elements. There's no place for it in the natural order of the world. Although I greatly appreciate plastic's utility, I dislike it aesthetically and try to have as little of it as possible in my home.

Plastic's greatest advantage, of course, is that it is very affordable compared to better-quality office accessories made of wicker, wood, glass, or metal. Even if you wanted to replace your plastic letter tray with a nice wood or leather one, perhaps that kind of upgrade is not in your budget right now. That's okay. Just add getting rid of some of the plastic stuff and replacing it with more natural materials to your list of future upgrades to make as your financial situation improves.

ACTION STEP

Look around your office for things made of plastic that you could easily replace with something composed of more natural elements. For example:

* Replace the plastic pencil holder on your desk with a wood, ceramic, glass, or metal container.

* Replace a plastic wastebasket with a wicker or metal design

* Use a leather or fabric cover for your checkbook, instead of that flimsy plastic one your bank gave you

* Get rid of that plastic mat under your desk chair unless you really need it; perhaps a small sisal rug would work as well

* Use ceramic or metal planters to hide the plastic containers your office plants are growing in

Activating Your Power Spots

Now that you know which elements are most helpful for your power spots—and which to minimize in those areas—it's time to choose or create a symbolic representation of your goal for each of your power spot *guas*.

You may feel inspired to use some typical feng shui cures, such as wind chimes, faceted crystal balls, or a water fountain to enhance your power spots, but these are by no means required. Before shopping for feng shui accessories, though, take a look at what you already have in your home. Items with personal meaning for you can be very effective feng shui enhancements.

CHOOSING SYMBOLIC OBJECTS AND IMAGERY

Feng shui symbols are visual reminders of the positive changes you wish to experience. The power they have comes from how you feel about them, so it's very important that you choose items and imagery that please and inspire you.

Keep the elements associated with your power spot *guas* in mind. What elements could you add to establish a Creative Cycle of energy? What colors, shapes, and imagery are associated with those elements?

Look through your possessions for objects and pictures that evoke appropriate associations for your specific goals and for the *gua* you are enhancing. What represents prosperity or success to you? What images make you feel balanced and calm, or strong and successful, or a leader in your community? What images represent creative fulfillment for you, a happy family life, deep contentment and inner peace?

You may already have a perfect object or image available in your office or elsewhere in your home, and all you have to do is move it to a more effective spot.

Visual imagery is especially powerful in triggering an emotional association or response, so it's important to be thoughtful about the symbolism of the pictures and images on display in your office. Make sure that they are positive and encouraging to you. Avoid any images that imply conflict, difficulty, or danger, as these qualities are not likely to be those you would like to associate with your business experience.

A dramatic photograph of a person scaling a mountain peak may be inspirational to some, but mountain climbing is a difficult and dangerous undertaking. Do you really want your business accomplishments to be "hard-won" or would it be nicer to allow them to come easily to you? On the other hand, if you are a climber, or your dream of success is to be able to take several months away from your business to go mountaineering in Nepal, this image would be appropriate for you.

Symbolism is extremely personal, and only you can make the final judgment of whether it lifts or lowers you spirits.If you aren't sure how an image is affecting you, use the muscle-testing method in Chapter 4 to assess your arm strength as you look at the pictures or objects in question.

MAKE A POWER SPOT COLLAGE

I hope you won't let lack of artistic talent stop you from making a feng shui symbol of your own, as this type of personal imagery can be very powerful. Among my favorite techniques is to make a collage of words and pictures representing the people, things, and experiences you wish to attract.

For example, if one of your goals is to reach Presidential Director level in your network marketing company, your collage might include a photograph from a recent newsletter showing someone else receiving that award: paste a photograph of you over that person's face, and write your own caption for the new image.

You can frame this collage and hang it in a power spot in your office—preferably where you will see it each time you enter the room or each time you look up from your desk. If you prefer not to put your hopes and dreams on public display, a good alternative is to make your collage on the inside of a file folder. Keep it where you can open it up and look at it frequently when you need a dose of inspiration.

The following pages present suggestions of appropriate imagery and accessories for each area of the *ba gua*. Use this information to help guide and inspire you as you activate your office power spots.

 *Career*

Kan gua is associated with WATER. Strengthen *kan gua* with:

* Dark blue or aqua for furnishings, upholstery and/or accessories such as curtains and pillows; black is also a water color—use it only as an accent color, because it is so dark

* Sinuous, curvy, irregular or wave-like shapes for furniture, fabric patterns, and decorative objects

* Water fountains and aquariums

* Photographs/imagery of waterfalls, rivers, lakes, ponds, ocean

* A wave machine, or a sound machine that reproduces the sound of a mountain stream, rain, or ocean waves

* METAL energy, to support WATER

WATER FOUNTAINS

An indoor water fountain is one of the most popular enhancements for *kan gua*. You can make a water fountain even more effective by building a Creative cycle of the elements around it.

* Choose a fountain with a ceramic bowl to represent EARTH, and place it on a METAL stand or table—or—choose a fountain with a METAL bowl, then add rocks or natural crystals (EARTH)

* Add greenery of some kind (WOOD) in or around the fountain, in the form of a living or artificial plant

* Add a touch of red—the color of FIRE and success; this could be a red cloth under the fountain, red flowers in a vase, or anything red that has appropriate personal meaning to you

* For a final touch, hang a beautiful, inspiring image on the wall above the fountain, or, hang a mirror there to reflect your image in the midst of all that powerful *chi*

CAREER IMAGERY

Kan gua is a good place for a picture that represents your career. For example, if you are a real estate agent, a photograph of you standing beside a FOR SALE sign for one of your listings would be appropriate here, especially if there's a big "SOLD" or "in escrow" sticker over the sign. If you are just starting out, find a photograph of a FOR SALE sign in front of the type of property you would like to represent, and paste your own picture into the photo.

PATH AND RIVER IMAGERY

If you are in or approaching a period of transition in your career path, activate *kan gua* with pictures of roads, paths, and rivers. Chose images that have a sense of destination to them so they won't represent a "road to nowhere." It's nice, too, if your image includes people, so you don't have to walk down your path alone.

 *Knowledge*

Ken gua is associated with EARTH. Strengthen *ken gua* with:

* Shades of brown, beige, yellow, and other EARTH tones for furnishings, upholstery, curtains and pillows
* Fabrics and textures that are soft and welcoming, inviting you to relax and settle your energy: corduroy, velvet, velour, cashmere, mohair, and chenille are all EARTH textures
* Ceramic vessels, tiles, and objects
* Large, heavy objects, such as statuary or stones
* Use lamps that shine down (table lamps or spot lighting) rather than uplights in this area, to match the settling quality of EARTH

EARTH is generated by FIRE, so a few red or triangular accents can be appropriate. Be careful not to add too much FIRE energy, however, as it may be over-stimulating and make it difficult to remain grounded and focused.

Ken gua is the area of learning and knowledge, so this part of your office is a good place to keep your reference books, and anything related to areas of current study. It is also associated with spirituality, specifically with meditation, retreat, and quiet introspection. Look for ways to evoke this aspect of *ken gua* with a statue or image of a religious figure appropriate to your spiritual practice.

This is not the best place for lots of activity and movement; mobiles and fans, for example, are best placed elsewhere in the room.*

 Family & Community

Jen gua is associated with young WOOD. Strengthen *jen gua* with:

* Living plants and flowers; use silk or other life-like artificial plants or flowers if maintenance is an issue

* Imagery of plants and gardens

* Pale to medium shades of green or blue for furnishings, upholstery, accessories

* Tall, narrow shapes and vertical stripes

* WATER energy, to nourish WOOD

Be sure to remove any unnecessary metal objects from *jen gua*, as METAL chops down WOOD.

Jen gua is the ideal place to celebrate your family heritage with a special photograph or memento. Do take care, though, not to bring too many images or objects from your personal life into your work space. Use *jen gua* of your home for your family photo gallery, and pick one favorite picture for *jen gua* in your office.

---

* *Remember, your goal is not to achieve perfection (which may not be possible); it is to do the best you can given the specific layout and restrictions of your space. If you need a fan to cool the room, and the only place for it is ken gua, don't fret about it. Just add some kind of earth-type energy nearby to help ground and stabilize the area.*

Images commemorating your community involvement are appropriate in *jen gua*, as are photos of you with any kind of work-related team you might be part of.

If you would like to be elected to an organization, find a photo of the group you would like to be a part of, and paste your picture into it.

WOOD imagery will be especially helpful here, as will all the shades of green that evoke new growth. Bamboo is a favored plant in feng shui because it grows and spreads rapidly, is flexible and strong, and is so versatile in its uses. Add some bamboo imagery to *jen gua* when you need to get moving on a new endeavor.

 *Wealth*

Hsun gua is associated with the energy of mature WOOD. Enhance *hsun gua* with:

- Dark green and purple furnishings, upholstery, and accessories

- Large plants, or plants with red or purple blossoms

- Money: coins or paper currency; any kind of imagery having to do with money and prosperity

- Wind chimes are a traditional enhancement for *hsun gua*

- Goldfish, either real ones in a tank or goldfish imagery

- Images of things that you are grateful for—the people, experiences, or material goods that are your "fortunate blessings"

- WATER energy, to nourish WOOD

MONEY TREE

Since *hsun gua* is associated with both WOOD and wealth *chi*, a "money tree" is a fun activation for this important *gua*. Here's how:

1. Place a good sized potted indoor tree (such as a ficus), real or life-like, in *hsun gua* of your office.

2. Every day, for 27 days, roll up a dollar bill, tie it with a 9" length of red string or ribbon, and hang it from a branch of your tree.

3. As you do this each day, keep your attention focused on the ever-increasing prosperity you intend to attract*

RICE BOWL

If you don't have space for an indoor tree in your office, here's an alternative enhancement that only takes up a little bit of room.

The use of rice as in blessing ceremonies and as a symbol of prosperity dates back to feng shui's roots in an agrarian culture. When the harvest is plentiful, the family has lots of food; when food is plentiful, the family is strong and healthy; when the family is strong and healthy, its members can work hard and prosper.

To make your own simple prosperity cure, fill a small bowl with uncooked rice, and stand or bury 3, 6, or 9 coins in the rice. Place the rice bowl in a prosperity power spot or on your home altar, with the intention that your wealth will grow and that you will reap a bountiful harvest of prosperity.

You can also write a specific prosperity wish, put it in a red envelope, and place the envelope underneath the rice bowl.

There's a great deal more involved in using feng shui to support increased prosperity than just enhancing the WEALTH area.

If financial security is a major concern, you may wish to make use of the more detailed information and advice available in *Fast Feng Shui for Prosperity: 8 Steps on the Path to Abundance*.

This title is available in ebook format at **FengShuiEbooks.com** and in softcover from **amazon.com** and other booksellers.

---

*   *Intention is powerful ingredient to feng shui. You'll learn about it in the next chapter.*

Fame

Li gua is associated with FIRE. Strengthen *li gua* with:

* Red, red, red—the brighter and bolder the better!

* Triangular shapes and pointed objects of any kind (be careful where you point them, though—you don't want to send secret arrows of *sha chi* flying around the office)

* Bright lights, red candles (use three or—even better—nine), twinkly little Christmas lights, red light bulbs

* Faceted crystal balls—use the biggest one you can afford

* A bright red telephone, to get people talking about you

* Upbeat, high-energy music

* WOOD energy, to nourish FIRE

FLOWER POWER

Red flowers are my favorite way to activate *li gua*, partly because I love flowers, but also because flowers represent the WOOD element, which feeds FIRE. There are many gorgeous red flowers you can use for feng shui enhancements: roses, carnations, geraniums, amaryllis, poinsettia, tulips, whatever is available in your climate and season.

If you use cut flowers to enhance *li gua*, use groupings of either three or nine blossoms. Change the water daily, and get rid of blossoms the instant they begin to wilt. Dying flowers are not good feng shui! For best effect, bring in new flowers every three days, so you have fresh flowers in place for a total of nine or 27 days.

STRUT YOUR STUFF

What do you want to be known for? *Li* is about fame and reputation, so take all those certificates, diplomas, and awards you are so proud of, and put them in *li gua*. Haven't made it big yet? Make up a mock award, press release, or magazine profile that applauds your future achievements, put it in a red frame, and hang it on the wall in *li gua*.

 *Relationships*

Kun gua is associated with the receptive, feminine, nurturing qualities of EARTH. While it is most associated with marriage and romantic partnerships, you can enhance *kun gua* to improve business alliances with:

● Luxurious accent pillows and soft fabrics

● Earth tones and/or shades of pink, white, and red

● Soothing, relaxing music

● Fragrant flowers with pink, white, or red blossoms

● Details and accents that evoke the energy of FIRE and EARTH

Some contemporary decorating styles make use of a lot of black, grey, and chrome. If you've chosen modern furniture for your office, make sure that you haven't added too much METAL energy to *kun gua*, as this will weaken EARTH. Look for subtle ways to add a soft touch, such as a beige rug under your sleek leather and chrome desk chair, or an abstract print with pastel and earth tones on the wall.

Strengthen existing business partnerships by placing a photograph of you and your partner(s) in *kun gua*. Be sure to choose a picture taken at a time when you were all happy and excited about the business and your future.

If you are looking for a new business associate, make a detailed list of the skills, experience, and personal qualities you are seeking, and keep this list in *kun gua* until you find the person it represents.

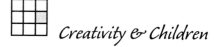 *Creativity & Children*

Dui gua is associated with METAL. Strengthen *dui gua* with:

● White and metallic colors/finishes for walls, furnishings, fabrics, and decorative accessories

● Round and oval shapes, arches

- Clean, simple, uncluttered spaces

- Natural and man-made crystals

- White flowers, plants with white blossoms

- EARTH element accents and details, to support METAL

CREATIVITY

Dui gua is the perfect place to celebrate the creative aspects of your business. Display or store your own artistic creations in *dui gua*, or keep your art books and supplies here. To activate your creativity, hang a faceted crystal ball over your head at your desk, keyboard, easel, or other work area in this part of the room.

Bright lights in *dui gua* encourage clear thinking and new ideas, but take care not to add too much FIRE energy, as it will melt the METAL *chi* of this area. A white votive candle can be used here to symbolize illumination and insight.

CHILDREN

Dui gua's association with children need not be taken literally in your work space unless your career specifically involves children in some way. For the rest of us, this area of the office is linked to the "children" of our business: employees or subordinates, if you have any, or your downline if you are involved in a network marketing business. If you want to expand your downline, be sure to get rid of clutter in this area and leave lots of room for growth.

 *Helpful Friends & Travel*

Like *dui*, *chien gua* is associated with METAL. Strengthen *chien gua* with:

- White and metallic colors/finishes for furnishings, fabrics, and accessories

- Round shapes

- Clean, simple, uncluttered spaces

- Natural and man-made crystals

- White flowers, plants with white blossoms

- EARTH element accents and details, to support METAL

HELPFUL FRIENDS

A strong *chien gua* indicates a strong support network, as well as lucky coincidences that bring you connections, information, or assistance with perfect timing.

Chien gua is not as high a priority for most people as the CAREER, WEALTH, or FAME areas. However, if your primary objective involves other people in any way (and if you think about it, it will), it's a good idea to activate *chien gua* to support your other efforts.

For example, activating *chien gua* can help attract:

- A good financial advisor

- The friend who faxes you an article on a company that turns out to be your next best customer

- The person you meet at a party who can help you get that business loan

YOUR VIRTUAL BOARD OF DIRECTORS

If you could recruit anyone—from any period of history—to sit on a Board of Directors for your business, who would you recruit to share their wisdom, perspective, and advice? Think about your own strengths and weaknesses, and be sure to include people with personalities and experiences that will complement what you have to offer. Aim for a list of 6-8 names for your "Virtual Board of Directors."

Create a document on a piece of white cardstock or posterboard, that includes a picture of each member of your VBoD, that person's name, and the position you have chosen each one to occupy, such as:

- "Director of Global Expansion"

- "Director of Positive Thinking"

- "Director of Right Livelihood"
- "Director of Innovative Marketing," etc.

Feel free to make up whatever positions you want. Give this document the title "Virtual Board of Directors for [*your company name*]" and display it in *chien gua* of your office.

TRAVEL

Chien gua is also associated with travel—which requires a lot of "helpful friends" in the guise of travel agents, airline, hotel, and rental car personnel. If you travel frequently, or are planning a trip, it's worth taking a look at *chien gua* to help everything go smoothly through the timely intervention of others.

If you travel excessively, and would like to spend less time on the road, add WATER and FIRE energy to *chien* to help control the METAL element.

 Tai Chi

Remember how we talked about how whatever happens in the *tai chi* of your home will affect all of the *guas* and all aspects of your life? This is true within your office as well. If you can, try to keep this area of the room open, rather than occupied by furniture.

If you have no choice but to place a piece of furniture in the *tai chi* of your office, be sure to also use one of the following remedies.

You can strengthen and activate the *tai chi* with:

- A faceted crystal ball or wind chime, hung from a red cord, string, or ribbon cut to a multiple of nine inches.
- Natural crystals or geodes
- A vase of fresh flowers
- Any very special personal imagery or objects

Activating the *tai chi* with a faceted crystal ball can have a powerful effect. It's a good addition to a room that could use more *yang* energy. If you are feeling stressed and overly busy, however, a vase of flowers will add vital energy to this area without overstimulating your office.

Other items to avoid in the *tai chi* include:

* Any kind of clutter (clutter here will block the energy of your entire office)

* A clock in the *tai chi* may contribute to time-related stress, feeling that you are always "racing the clock" to get things done

Although the *tai chi* is associated with the EARTH element, this is an excellent place for an object, image, or grouping of items that represents all five of the elements, to ensure balance and harmony among all five aspects or qualities of *chi*.

ACTION STEPS

1. Decide on a specififc enhancement for each of your power spot *guas*. This should be an object or image that has an appropriate symbolic meaning to you.

2. Evaluate the element balance of that area of the room. Is the element of that *gua* adequately supported?

   If not, what element(s) do you need to add to create productive cycle or strengthen the native element of that *gua*?

   Think in terms of materials, shapes, colors, and imagery.

3. Plan how you will combine the necessary element adjustments with your planned enhancement.

   For example, choose a metal or wood picture frame and/or the color of the frame as appropriate for that area of the *ba gua*.

The Ba Gua of Your Desk

Yes, the *ba gua* can be applied to your desk, just as it can to any defined area. WEALTH, FAME, and RELATIONSHIPS are at the far side from where you sit at the CAREER area of the desk.

This does not mean, however, that you should clutter up your desk with feng shui accessories, or place things in inconvenient spots just because that's where they fit the *ba gua*. Maintaining the integrity of your work surface for work is important! Be wary of one-size-fits-all advice such as "keep your address book in the HELPFUL FRIENDS area of your desk." This might work if you are following the compass *ba gua*, and *ken gua* is out of the way, but it is more likely to be hugely inconvenient. Keep your address book wherever makes function sense for you, and don't worry about where it is according to the *ba gua*.

If you like the idea of using the *ba gua* of your desk, have a piece of glass cut to size to cover the desktop. Then slip photographs, post-cards, collages, or other imagery of symbolic importance to you under the glass where it will not be in your way. How far you go with this is up to you. You could turn your entire desktop into a *ba gua* collage if you wanted to—but you might find that two or three carefully chosen images have greater impact.

ACTION STEP

The best feng shui for your desktop is to keep it tidy and uncluttered.

* What items do you habitually keep on your desk?

* Do they allow you enough room to work comfortably?

* Do you use them all on a daily basis?

Make sure every item on your desk is there for a reason.

Guas within Guas

By now you have looked at the *ba gua* of your house, the *ba gua* of your office, and even the *ba gua* of your desk. Take a moment now to look for any significant areas of overlap that you could take advantage of. If your office is in *hsun gua* (WEALTH) of your house, for example, then the WEALTH area within your office has extra emphasis.

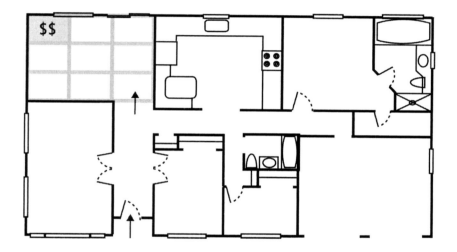

To take it one step further, the WEALTH area of a piece of furniture that happens to be in *hsun gua* of your office, will be a potent focus for WEALTH energy, and a good place for a symbol that represents achievement of your *hsun gua* goal.

Let's say your WEALTH goal is to increase your income by 30% this year. Think of a visual image that represents what you'd like to experience as a *result* of achieving that goal: for example, maybe you plan to celebrate with a weekend in Las Vegas when you reach your income target. You could write your name, income goal, and target travel dates on a picture of the hotel you'd like to stay at, and put that in your *hsun gua* super-power spot. A visual image like this can help you imagine your desired outcome more clearly, and that's important, as you will learn in Chapter 7.

ACTION STEP

Find the area of your office that matches the location of your office within the *ba gua* of your home. (For example, if your office is in the CREATIVITY area of your home, locate the CREATIVITY area within your office.)

* What area of the house does your office occupy?

* Where is that *gua* within your office?

* Look for something in that area that defines a smaller, discrete area to which the *ba gua* could be applied (For example, the top of a table, desk, or cabinet, or a shelf in a bookcase.)

  If nothing obvious is present in that area, consider moving a side table to that area, or affixing a display shelf to the wall there, to enable you to take advantage of this method.

* Now, find the same *gua* on that shelf or table top. This is a powerful spot for the energy of that *gua*.

* What was your goal for this *gua*? (Refer to your answers to the action steps on page 192 where you defined a specific aspiration for each *gua*.)

* Choose something—an object or image—that symbolizes your goal, that you can place in the super-duper-power spot you've identified. This could be a small object, a picture, or you can write your goal on a piece of paper that is an appropriate color for that *gua*.

  Your symbolic item does not have to be on display: it can go inside a drawer, behind a picture frame, or even between the pages of a book in that area.

Focal Points

Our focus in this chapter has been on your "power spots" as defined by the *ba gua*. However, there are at least two more areas of your office that deserve special attention: the first thing that attracts your attention when you enter your office, and whatever you look at when you are seated at your desk.

Both of these focal points will have a strong effect on your energy and mood, so make sure that whatever is in those areas sends a postive message! For example, if the first thing you see when you walk through the office door is a pile of old project files that should have been tossed or put away long ago, the energy of that unfinished but outdated business will affect your ability to focus fully on your current projects and assignments.

While you are at your desk, pay attention to what catches your eye when you aren't looking at the computer screen—such as when talking on the phone, for example. Your *chi* goes where your attention goes, so choose an inspiring image, object, or symbol, and place it where it will catch your attention when you are at your desk.

You may be able to combine these important focal points with remedies or enhancements for one of your power spots, depending on the layout of your office.

ACTION STEP

Create two specific focal points in your office: to catch your eye as you enter the office, and when you sit at your desk. You might use an image or artwork hung on the wall, a figurine on a shelf, or an object on a windowsill. Whatever you choose should be attractive and pleasing to the eye—if you can also incorporate personal symbolic meaning, that's even better. Simple items can be very effective, and you can change your selection as often as you want. What's going to motivate and inspire you today?

Final Check

Variety, it is said, is the spice of life. The more hours you spend in your office each day, the more important it is that this space is stimulating as well as comfortable. Take a look at your office as a whole now, to make sure that the furniture, equipment, and décor of the room includes:

- At least one item that is in motion. This could be: the blades of a fan; the leaves of a plant in front of an open window; a mobile or other kinetic art; a water fountain; or the second hand on your wall clock.

- Something that contributes living *chi*, such as a potted plant, vase of fresh flowers, or an aquarium or goldfish bowl.

  If this is not possible for your space or lifestyle, incorporate some kind of natural imagery that is as lifelike as possible, such as nature photography.

- At least one item that represents each of the five elements: WATER, WOOD, FIRE, EARTH, and METAL.

  The elements do not have to be represented equally, but each should be present in some way.

  Incorporating these influences into your office decor will give the space greater vitality. You will find that you feel more comfortable in the room, with increased energy and alertness as you tend to the business of working at home.

There's one final ingredient to the feng shui of your home office, and that is your own *chi* as demonstrated in your thoughts, feelings, and behaviors. You'll learn some easy ways to put that to use in the next—and final—chapter…

7

The Secret
Ingredient

*F*eng shui works from the inside out as much as it works from the outside in. Sometimes we focus so much on how our environment is affecting us that we forget that our own physical presence and emotional state are major influences on the energy of our space. This means that *how* you place the feng shui symbols and remedies you chose for your home office is as important as *where* you decide to place them.

Feng shui symbols are visual reminders of the positive changes you wish to experience; the power they have comes from how you feel about them. If you are worried about money and decide to place a wealth symbol in *hsun gua*, it's important to do so with a positive outlook. That symbol should remind you that you expect improvements in your finances to be coming along any moment now. If you feel this with confidence, your confident expectation helps fuel the success of the feng shui remedy.

Confident expectation means releasing anxiety about your income or unpaid bills or how difficult it may be feeling right now to attract the new clients you need to grow your business. It means not getting too distracted by the "reality" of your present situation, and trusting absolutely that things are already starting to improve for you, even if you can't see any evidence of it yet.

If you place your wealth symbol while worrying about money, and every time you look at that symbol it triggers doubts such as, "Why isn't it working yet?," "How am I ever going to get out of debt?," or "I really need this to work; our money situation is looking really bad," your focus on worries and problems fuels the downside of your situation and keeps you in a state of lack.

This is true no matter what your focus is, or which area of your home you are working on. If you are placing romance symbols in your bedroom, for example, thoughts about how lonely you feel, how desperately you wish to meet someone, or how hurt you were by a past breakup will undermine the effectiveness of your feng shui by filling the space with the energy of loneliness, heartache, and regret.

WORRYING IS LIKE ASKING FOR WHAT YOU DON'T WANT

Many of the emails I receive from people seeking feng shui advice are written from a state of anxiety or hopelessness (this is especially true where issues of work or money are involved). "I really hope you can help me, because I am feeling desperate," is a common refrain.

What many people fail to understand is that the best feng shui advice in the world can only do so much if your emotional atmosphere is polluted with worry and discouragement. Consciously focusing your energy on what you want to experience, rather than on what you *don't* want—with belief that it can and will manifest for you—is critical to your success with feng shui.

When life throws challenges your way, keeping this positive focus can be difficult. It is easy to get so caught up in worry that we forget that thinking and feeling positively is a choice. What has most helped me get through difficult times in my own life is the reminder that "Worrying is like asking for what you don't want." I've learned, when I feel anxious about something, to recognize anxiety as a sign that I have allowed my thoughts and feelings to pull me in the wrong direction and it's time to refocus on intending a better future for myself.

YOUR CLARITY OF INTENTION IS THE KEY TO SUCCESS

The strategies you've learned in this book are just one aspect of the energy shifts that will bring you greater success in your home-based business; the rest arise from your attitude and expectation and from your willingness to make whatever behavioral changes might also be required. Remember, the foremost principle of feng shui is that everything is connected. When you hope that a feng shui object or symbol will solve problems for you, without requiring any other effort on your part, you abdicate your power to the object and leave yourself out of the energy dynamic in your home.

A more effective approach is to select feng shui symbols not for what they are supposed to do *for* you, but by how powerfully they encourage and inspire you. Then, place these symbols or objects in your office as reminders to maintain a positive outlook as you take inspired action to improve your circumstances.

Each time you see that symbol or object, pause for a moment to visualize your desired outcome and imagine that it is already happening for you. When you imbue your own positive and optimistic energy into your symbols in this way, you empower them to assist you. This distinction between abdicating (giving up) your power to a symbol, and imbuing (saturating) it with your intention is one of the most important concepts in contemporary feng shui.

The role of feng shui images and objects is not to do the work for you. It's to inspire you to accomplish greater things, with greater ease, faster than you would on your own, by using your focused intention and optimism to create an environment that resonates with vitality, success, prosperity, and the joy and satisfaction of knowing your dreams have come true.

The strength and clarity of your intention to initiate positive change in your life is an integral part of your success with feng shui. When you dwell on how dissatisfied you are with a life situation, your energy becomes stuck there. Approach feng shui with confidence, optimism, and a sense of adventure. This will keep you motivated, and will help to shift the energy of your home.

Here's an easy method to help you do that.

The "IVAG" Empowerment Process

What is "empowerment"? It is a specific method that you can use each time you place a feng shui cure or enhancement in your home or office with the intention of improving the feng shui of your space. It reinforces external changes with the power of your thoughts and feelings about the results that you desire to experience in your life.

The empowerment method given here greatly enhances your efforts by focusing the power of your body, speech and mind on what you are doing. In my first two *Fast Feng Shui* books, I taught this method as I had learned it, using just the Intention, Visualization, and Affirmation steps. Over the years, however, I have become more and more convinced that Gratitude is the most important factor of all. With this in mind, I now include Gratitude as a fourth step in the empowerment process.

MUDRAS AND MANTRAS

When making any feng shui adjustments, you may wish to use the "dispelling mudra"* nine times while repeating the mantra, *om mani padme hum*, nine times. The mudra, or hand gesture, represents the power of body; the mantra is the power of speech, and visualizing your desired outcome while you use the mantra and mudra uses the power of mind.

These buddhist traditions are very powerful, and can work for anyone, regardless of your religious background. (If you would prefer to use a prayer or mantra from your own spiritual tradition, that is absolutely acceptable. Always be guided by what feels best for you.)

The mudra and mantra can be used in combination with the "IVAG" method:

---

* *Hold your index and pinky fingers straight and curl your middle and ring finger toward the palm, holding them with your thumb. (Women, use your right hand; men use your left hand.) Now flick the middle and ring fingers out to dispel negative energy from whatever you have flicked at.*

1.   INTENTION: As you are making feng shui changes to your space, stay focused on your intention that these changes will have a positive effect on your circumstances.

2.   VISUALIZATION: Visualize your desired outcome in your mind, as if it has already taken place.

     Be as detailed and concrete as possible; visualize a specific experience and use all of your senses, so you actually feel the happiness, satisfaction, or relief that you expect your desired results to bring.

3.   AFFIRMATION: Make a verbal affirmation—in the present tense—that clearly states the intended shift in your energy and/or circumstances.

     If you don't wish to say your affirmation aloud, it's okay to whisper it or to say it subvocally. Some people may find it helpful to write their affirmation and read it aloud; seeing the affirmation in writing is another way of involving the visual sense.

4.   GRATITUDE: End your empowerment with a few moments of heartfelt gratitude.

     Imagine that everything you desire has been achieved. Enlist your power of imagination and visualization again, and really feel as though your desired outcome has been achieved, and it's even better than you had anticipated!

     You will know you are doing this step correctly if there's a smile on your face. There may even be a few tears of joy in your eyes as well. Welcome them, and express your thanks for all of your desired blessings as though you have already received them.

Steps 1-3 may be done in any order, or simultaneously. You can also place your cures (with intention) at any convenient time, then do steps 2 through 4 at another time. During the hours of 11 AM to 1 PM, and 11 PM to 1 AM, the energy of the day is shifting; these are good times to empower feng shui changes. If you follow Chinese or western astrology, you may use either of these systems to choose an auspicious day and time for your empowerments.

Blessing Your Space

A ritual or ceremony to bless your office is entirely optional. If you like the idea of doing this, please feel free to do so in any way that you choose. Blessing ceremonies are an integral part of every culture, so you may be familiar with or inspired to follow a ritual that is very different from the one I present here.

For those who are interested in a blessing ceremony that is specific to the style of feng shui that you have learned in this book, here are instructions for a practice called "Tracing the Nine-Star Path," which is based on the nine areas of the *ba gua*.

The original ceremony is designed to be used for your entire house (and you can do it that way, if you wish); I have adapted these instructions to apply just to your home office.

Tracing the 9-Star Path

This blessing method is appropriate for any space. It will adjust and activate the *chi* of your home office and bless the space with good luck.

SUPPLIES NEEDED:

* An attractive piece of cloth to cover your desktop; this could be a tablecloth or shawl, or simply a piece of fabric. Choose something that feels ceremonial or special to you in some way. Use your best tablecloth for this ceremony, rather than the old one you drag out for picnics.

* A bouquet of fresh flowers in a pretty vase. These flowers should be purchased (or picked from your garden) specifically for this ceremony. It is best—but not essential—that the flowers be fragrant.

* 3 sticks of incense

* An incense burner (or, place half an orange cut-side-down on a glass or ceramic plate; with an ice pick or skewer, poke three holes in the top of the orange and insert the incense sticks into these holes)

- Nine red envelopes (these can be any size, but must be new; the small Chinese red envelopes traditional for New year are a good choice and are just the right size to hold a business-card sized piece of paper.

- Small pieces of paper on which to write your blessing wishes

- A red pen

- A small bowl of uncooked rice

- *Optional*: a candle, bell, spiritual figurine or image, faceted feng shui crystal, etc.—whatever sacred objects or other items you feel inspired to include   .

PREPARATION

Think of a specific wish or blessing for each of the life aspirations represented by the *ba gua*.

1) Family & Community

2) Wealth

3) Balance (*tai chi*)

4) Helpful Friends & Travel

5) Creativity & Children

6) Knowledge

7) Fame

8) Career

9) Relationships

Write your blessing or wish for each life aspect on a small piece of paper using the red pen. As you do this, visualize specifically how you wish this to manifest for you. If you and a partner are defining your wishes separately, you should each use your own set of papers.

Clear everything off your desk and cover the desktop with the cloth. Place the flower vase, red envelopes, written wishes, and any other ceremonial items you are including on the desk.

PROCEDURE

1.   Light the candle (if you are using one) and the incense. Make sure that they are placed where they will burn safely while your attention is elsewhere during the ceremony.

2.   Ring a bell, if you have one, or hold a moment of silent prayer to begin the ceremony. Imagine your office is ready and eager for your blessing. If you like, call upon gods, saints or guides from your spiritual practice to be with you and assist you in the ceremony.

3.   State aloud your intention to bless your office and welcome in joy and prosperity for yourself, your business, your family, and everyone involved.

4.   Take one of the red envelopes and put into it a generous pinch of the rice. Find your written wish or blessing for "family & community" and take it and the red envelope with the rice in it that area of your office.

5.   Read your wish for that *gua* aloud. If partners have written separate wishes, each person should read in turn. (Anyone who wants to keep a wish private should not be required to share it.)

6.   Place the written wish paper(s) into the red envelope, then place the envelope somewhere in that area where it can remain for several weeks undisturbed. This can be in plain view, inside a drawer or box, or even taped to the back of a picture or mirror.

7.   Take a moment to visualize your desired outcome for that aspect of your life in as much detail as possible. Try to actually feel the joy and satisfaction you will experience when your wishes come true, as you make the dispelling mudra and recite the *om mani padme hum* mantra nine times (see page 228).

8.   Return to your desk, and repeat these steps for the WEALTH area. Continue through each of the nine *guas* in the exact sequence they are listed on page 231. Note that this is a different order than the simple clockwise circuit of the *ba gua* that I have used earlier in this book.

9. When all of the envelopes have been placed, enjoy a few moments of silent prayer as you visualize success, joy and wellbeing filling the entire office.

10. If you are using a bell, ring it again to close the ceremony.

FOLLOW-UP

Leave the envelopes in place for 27 days. If you like, you can return daily to each of the nine areas and use the dispelling mudra and Six True Words mantra, visualizing all your wishes and blessings coming true.

On the 28th day, collect all the envelopes and place them in a special place in the "fortunate blessings" area (*hsun gua*; WEALTH) of your office, or you may burn them.

Embracing Change

We often think of feng shui as a method for fixing things that have gone wrong in our lives. We expect change to be something that we will go through in order to get what we want, at which point we'll be happy and content. But change is constant; it is what life is about.

Stasis, in feng shui terms, means stagnation. In a state of truly perfect balance and harmony, there's no room for vitality and experience. That's why the *tai chi* symbol shows a little bit of the opposite within each side of the duality, and why as one side reaches its strongest expression the other begins to emerge.

This ancient symbol is a powerful representation of the constant change and evolution that is inherent to life itself.

As the feng shui adjustments that you have made to your home office assist you in achieving your goals, new directions will beckon to you and your priorities will shift and change, perhaps dramatically. It is right and appropriate that your feng shui enhancements will change as well.

Plan to revisit the life aspirations of the *ba gua* periodically as your business grows and your interests and objectives evolve along with your life direction. Then evaluate whether any of your personal symbols have served their purpose and can be retired or replaced.

I wish you success and satisfaction in your home-based business, and hope that it brings great joy and prosperity to you and your family,

aloha,

Stephanie Roberts

Appendix

Drawing a Floor Plan

Defining the Compass Sectors

The Modern Ba Gua

Drawing a Floor Plan

If you do not have a floor plan of your house or apartment, and need to create one of your own, here are some guidelines for how to do it. Accuracy is important, so don't guess or estimate. Free-hand sketches and approximations should not be used for feng shui purposes; you could end up making important decisions based on inaccurate information or placement. Please do yourself a favor and take the time to do it right.

You will need:
* some free time
* a pad of ¼" graph paper
* a pencil and eraser
* a good quality tape measure (a metal one from the hardware store, not a dressmakers tape)
* a ruler to make drawing straight lines easier
* tape for taping pieces of paper together

Work in pencil so you can correct mistakes, then go over the final version with a black medium-point pen. You may use a computer drawing program, but you'll still need to physically walk around your home measuring and recording dimensions, and the best way to do that is on your graph paper pad.

Don't worry about being accurate to the inch, but do be sure that the scale is consistent, and the following features are included:
* all exterior and interior walls (including closets)
* doors & windows in any room you might use for your office
* stairs
* major appliances (stove, refrigerator, TV, A/C unit, etc.)
* location of fusebox and electric meter

If your home has more than one level, you'll need a separate page for each floor.

1. Decide what scale you are going to use: if you are using 1/4"
    grid paper, you might choose to have one small square equal to
    half a foot (6") when you measure a room.

2. Decide where to start. A corner room is good. Measure the length
    and width of the room, convert inches or feet into squares on
    your graph paper, and draw the outline of that room on your
    paper. Add the door, and mark where the windows are.

3. Go to whatever room or hallway is next to the one you started
    with, and measure that one with your tape measure. Convert
    inches and feet into little squares on your paper, and outline
    that space. Add doors and windows, and move on.

4. Unless you are very left-brain oriented and have planned care-
    fully, you probably run out of space on your sheet of paper.
    That's okay. Tape a fresh piece of paper to the one you started
    with, and keep going.

If you have a large home and have created an unwieldy mess of
taped-together papers—and have not yet run out of patience— you
can make a cleaner, neater version at a smaller scale. Using your
first draft as a guide, redraw your layout, making each little square
on your graph paper equal to a greater measure this time. For example, if your first version had a 1/4" square equal to 6" in real
measure, you could now use a 1/4" square to equal one or two feet,
or whatever scale is most useful for you.

If you can keep the entire outline of your home under 11"x17", that's
great, because any good copy shop will be able to duplicate that
size for you. If your home is not particularly grand, you can probably get a basic outline onto a standard (8-1/2"x11") or legal size
(8-1/2"x14") piece of paper.

Now you are ready to have photocopies made. Be sure to keep one
copy clean and unmarked, in case you need to make more duplicates later.

Defining the Compass Sectors

Some practitioners recommend using the grid method for the compass *ba gua*, because it's easy and divides the interior of the home into equal sections. However, this method can be inaccurate unless your home is closely aligned to the mid-point of one of the eight compass sectors used in feng shui. (See pages 60-61 for an example.)

If you want to use the nine-unit grid for your home, stick with the doorway method. If you want to follow the compass directions for your *ba gua*, use the "pie slice" or "wedge" method as described here.

One thing you will notice about this method is that—unless you live in a circular home, which few people do—the areas covered by the different sectors are not of equal size. The larger *guas* will have a stronger influence on the spaces they cover. Smaller *guas* are considered weaker.

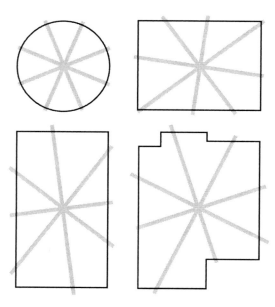

FIND THE PHYSICAL CENTER OF YOUR HOME

Before you can divide your floor plan into compass sectors, you need to find the center of your house or apartment.

If the main floor of your home is a tidy rectangle, this is easy to do: just draw diagonal lines connecting opposite corners. The point where the lines cross is the center of the home:

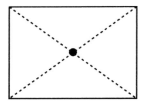

If your home is basically rectanglar, with a few irregularities, this simple method can still be used:

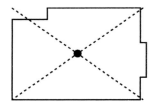

If your home is a trapeziod (one end of the house is fatter than the other), nudge the center point slightly toward the fatter side:

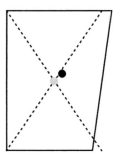

If your home is L-shaped, look at it as two separate rectangles, and find the center of each. Connect the two centers and find the mid-point of that line, then nudge it toward the larger section of the house. How much of a nudge depends on the difference in size between the two sections:

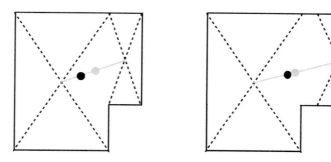

If the outline of your home is a more irregular shape, but can still be divided into two distinct sections, you can use this same method to find the center point:

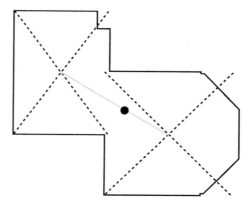

If your house has more than two sections, connecting the center point of the various areas will create a three, four, or more-sided shape (see diagrams, next page).

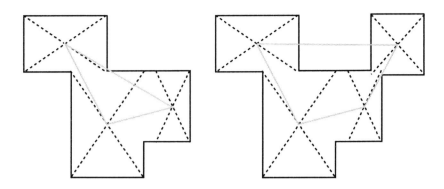

Find the center of this new shape. For a triangle, connect each point to the center of the opposite side. For a trapezoid, connect the centers of opposing sides:

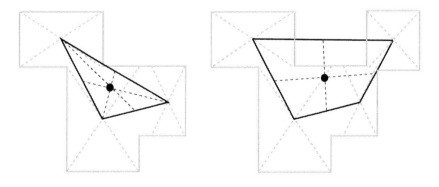

Nudge the center point slightly toward the largest section:

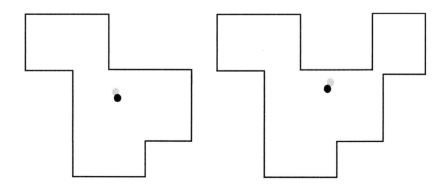

If your home can't be easily divided into sections, use this alternative method:

First, cut around the outline of your house/apartment.

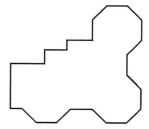

Push a straight pin through the paper cut-out, very close to one corner (or the closest thing you've got to a corner). Hold the paper up by the pin, and allow the paper to hang however it wants.

Grab the bottom point or side of the shape with your free hand and lay the cutout carefully down on the table. Use a ruler or other straight edge and a pencil to draw a vertical line from "top" to "bottom" of the shape. Repeat two more times at other points:

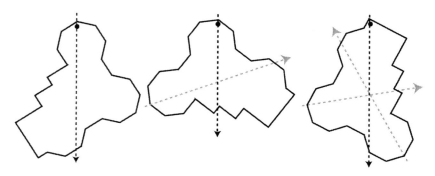

The point or area where those three lines cross is the physical center of your home.

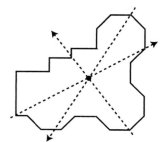

FINDING THE COMPASS SECTORS

Once you have marked your floor plan with the center point, you are ready to divide it into compass sectors.

Each sector is 45° wide, and is centered on one of the compass directions (**N, NE, E, SE, SW, W, NW**).

Take care, when you are marking the compass sectors on your floor plan, to *center* the sectors on the compass directions, rather than lining up the sector dividing lines with the compass lines:

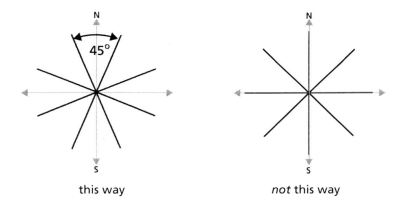

this way   *not* this way

Start by marking where North is on your floor plan. If you have a builder's or architect's plan for your home, look for a small arrow somewhere on the page indicating North. Draw a parallel line through the center point of your home.

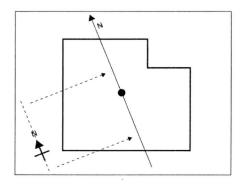

The arrow printed on your floor plan is probably accurate enough for this purpose, although I did work with one client whose builder's plan was off by 180° (the arrow supposed to indicate North was actually showing South). You may wish to take a compass reading of your own to be sure.

If you are taking your own compass reading, follow these steps:

1. Figure out what direction one side of your house faces (any side will do, whatever's convenient):

    For a house, take your reading outside. Stand facing the house.

    For an apartment, stand inside, facing an exterior wall.

    Make sure you are facing the wall squarely, not turned slightly to one side or the other.

    Hold the compass level and wait for the needle to stop spinning. Turn the dial so "0" (North) is directly lined up with the main end of the needle (compasses vary, but this will be marked in some way).

    Read the degree mark that lines up with the vertical line on the compass:

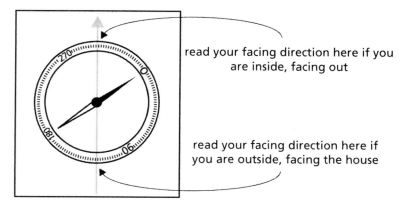

read your facing direction here if you are inside, facing out

read your facing direction here if you are outside, facing the house

    This is the "facing direction" of that side of your house. For this example, we'll say our facing direction is **304°**.

Because EMF fields can distort compass readings, it's a good idea to take readings at several different spots. Probably there will be some variation. Make your best guess based on the readings you get.

2. Mark that direction on your floor plan.

    In pencil, draw a line through the center of your house through the side you took the compass reading for. Write the compass reading beside the line.

    Mark another arrow indicating North (0°). (The compass degrees run clockwise from 0 to 360, which are the same point.)

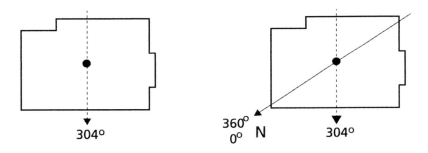

3. Now divide your floor plan into eight equal sectors. Make sure the sectors are centered on the **N-S** line (see page 244). Label the sectors (**N, NE, E, SE, S, SW, W, NE**).

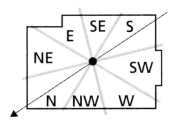

If you don't trust yourself to draw the lines by eye, use the drawing program on your computer to draw a large 90° cross.

Copy and paste a second cross on top of the first one, and rotate it 45°.

Your drawing should look like this:

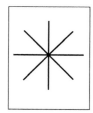

Print it out, and tape it to a sunny window. Hold your floor plan on top of it, turning it so the center of the crosses line up with the center point of your floor plan and the N-S line is in the center of one of the sectors.

Mark or trace the sector lines onto your floor plan and label the sectors with the compass directions.

THE COMPASS SECTORS FOR A ROOM

To find the compass sectors for a room, follow the same steps described above. This time you will:

1. Find the center point of the room.

2. Find where North is relative to that room.

3. Mark the North line through the center point of the room.

4. Mark the compass sectors, remembering to *center* the sectors on the N-S line (page 244).

5. Label the sectors.

It takes pages of instructions to explain how to do this, but once you grasp the concepts involved it's really not very difficult. It's worth taking the time to do this right so you have an accurate map of the compass sectors for your home and can know for sure which areas are lucky or unlucky for you, according to your *kua* number (see pages 68-71 in Chapter 2 for details).

The Modern Ba Gua

Contemporary western feng shui arranges the *ba gua* based on the main entry to a space (whether an entire building or an individual room) rather than by the compass directions. Follow these steps to determine the *ba gua* of your home based on the doorway.

The Ba Gua of a House

1. If your house has more than one level, start with the *ba gua* for the main floor.

    Turn your floor plan so the front door is at the bottom of the page, and the back of the house is at the top of the page.

    Even if you usually enter your home through the garage or a back or side door, always align the *ba gua* to the formal main entry. "Main entry" here is determined by architectural prominence, not by which door you and your family use most often.

2. Draw a line across the page at the door. Some parts of your house (often the garage) may stick out in front of the door. That's okay. For now, just mark the door line:

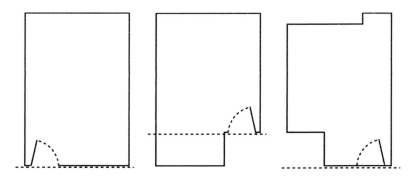

3. Draw a nine-unit grid covering the length and width of the area of the house that is *behind* the front door:

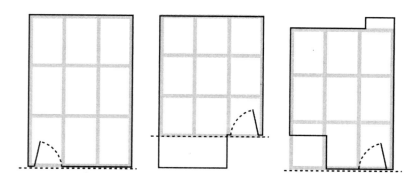

WHAT TO DO ABOUT THE ODD BITS STICKING OUT

If the outline of your home or apartment is not a neat rectangle, you may not be sure where the outside lines of the *ba gua* should go. Here are some guidelines for fine-tuning your *ba gua* placement.

- **Porches & Carports**

  The *ba gua* only covers interior spaces—rooms that are fully enclosed with a roof and exterior walls. A covered porch or carport is not part of the *ba gua*, because at least one side is open.

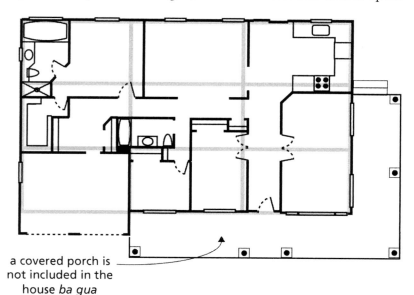

a covered porch is not included in the house *ba gua*

- **Garages**

   An attached garage which has a direct entry into the house is included in the house *ba gua*.

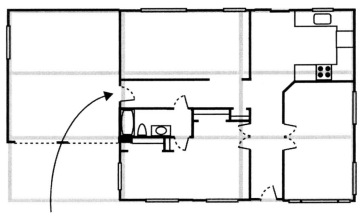

This garage offers access to the house;
   it is included in the house *ba gua*

However, if your garage is detached or if it does not provide direct access into the house, it is considered a separate structure (even if it shares a wall with the house) and is not included in the house *ba gua*. In this case the garage has its own *ba gua*.

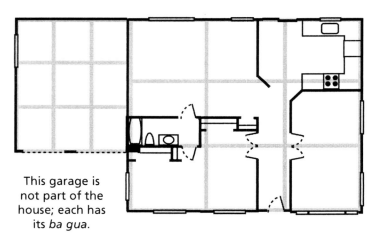

This garage is
not part of the
house; each has
   its *ba gua*.

● **Recessed Entry**

Always place the *ba gua* so the lower edge is right at the front door. For homes with a recessed entry, this means that some parts of the house are "outside" the *ba gua*.

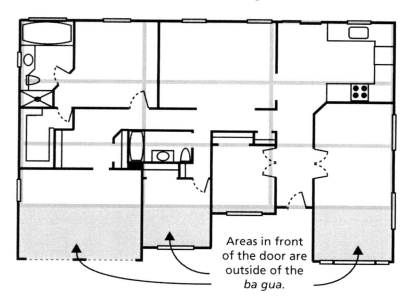

Areas in front of the door are outside of the *ba gua*.

● **Protruding Entry**

In some cases, the entry itself sticks out from the rest of the home (this is more common in apartments than houses).

Here, some parts of the *ba gua* itself are outside the home.

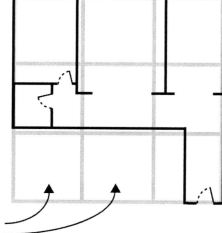

parts of this *ba gua* are outside the boundaries of the home

- **Extensions & Missing Areas**

  An **extension** is a part of the home that sticks out from the basic shape of the structure. It increases the energy of the *gua(s)* it extends beyond, and is considered a good thing:

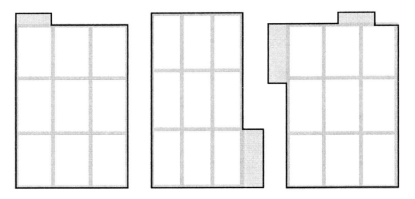

  A **missing area** is like a bite taken out of the basic shape of the house. It weakens the energy of the affected *gua(s)*, and is considered a drawback (see Chapter 5 for suggested remedies):

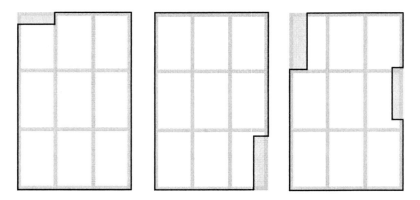

  It's not always clear whether you've got an extension (good) or a missing area (not good). Here's how to tell the difference:

At the **front** of the house, the edge of the *ba gua* is always determined by the location of the doorway (see pages 248 and 251). Any part of the house that is *in front of* that line is an extension.

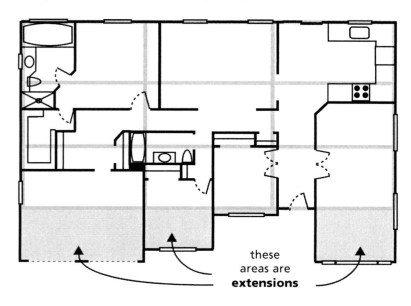

these
areas are
extensions

Where the *ba gua* covers an area outside the walls of the house those parts of the *ba gua* are "missing."

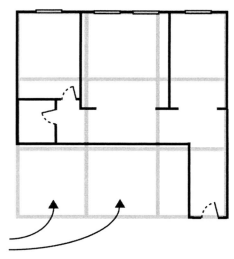

these
areas are
missing
from this
ba gua

On the **sides** or at the **back** of the house, measure the total length
of that side of the house; the longest section of wall defines the
boundary of the house *ba gua.*

In order to qualify as an **extension**, any part that sticks out must
be *less than* half the total length of that side of the house (diagram **A**, below). If it's more than half the total length it is covered by the *ba gua*, and what you've got is a missing area beside
it (diagram **B**):

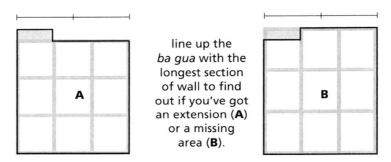

line up the
ba gua with the
longest section
of wall to find
out if you've got
an extension (**A**)
or a missing
area (**B**).

Similarly, a "bite" from the side or back of the house must be
less than half the total length of that side of the house (**B**). Otherwise the *ba gua* does *not* cover the "bite" (**A**) and what you've
got is an extention.

This odd shape is the outline of an apartment that I found at a
realtor's web site. It has two large extensions (**a**) and (**b**) and a
smaller missing area
(**c**) on the balcony.

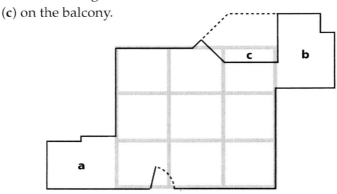

- **Homes with very irregular outlines**

   If your home has a very irregular shape, it may be difficult or impossible to tell whether you've got missing areas or extentions or both. This is one reason why simple, regular shapes are preferred in feng shui. The lack of clarity in terms of what *gua* is where may be reflected in a lack of mental or emotional clarity in some way for the occupants.

   Very irregular shapes have unbalanced *ba guas*, which implies imbalance in the energy of the home. This is not always a bad thing, however. Perfect balance implies stasis, or lack of movement and progress. Some dynamic tension is not a bad thing.

   In extreme cases, such as those shown below, using the doorway method for the *ba gua* may be impossible. If so, you can always go by the compass directions.

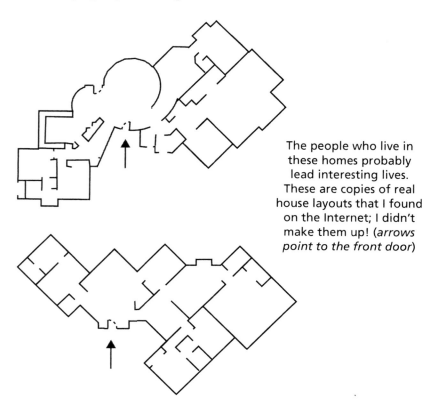

The people who live in these homes probably lead interesting lives. These are copies of real house layouts that I found on the Internet; I didn't make them up! (*arrows point to the front door*)

LEVELS ABOVE AND BELOW

There are conflicting opinions about how to use the doorway *ba gua* for levels above or below the main floor. In my first book, *Fast Feng Shui*, I shared the guidelines that I was taught in my feng shui classes: to use the top (for upper floors) or bottom (for lower floors) of the stairs as the "entry point" for that level.

This sounds fine, in theory, but in application it often results in extremely distorted *ba guas* that are of little practical use. As my own practice has developed, I now rarely apply the *ba gua* in this way.

Other feng shui writers and teachers say to just follow the *ba gua* for the main floor, so that a second-floor room above the CAREER area (*kan gua*) of the house, for example, is assumed to be in the CAREER area of that level... even though this may vary greatly from the "use the entry point at the top of the stairs" method.

Over the years, I've come to believe that there is no one definitive answer to this question. If the upper floors of your home have the same overall outline as the rest of your house, then it makes sense to use the same *ba gua* as for the main level. Where the "footprint" or basic shape of one level of the house is very different from the main level, however, I believe it should be treated separately.

In most cases, however, I don't use an overall *ba gua* at all for upper (or lower) levels. This is because in most homes the public and shared spaces—those used by all family members, and that are seen by visitors to the home—are on the main level.

Other levels are usually made up of the private spaces of the family's bedrooms and bathrooms. Bedrooms are by their nature private spaces, which means that the *ba gua* of that room is more important than where that room is within the *ba gua* of the house or of that level of the house.

I pay close attention to the main floor *ba gua*, and on other levels I just look at the *ba gua* of the individual room.

THE BA GUA FOR AN APARTMENT

An apartment, by definition, is a private unit within a larger structure. You can, if you wish, look at what *gua* your apartment occupies within the *ba gua* of the building as a whole, to get a sense of what flavor that might impart to the energy of your home. I don't believe this is a strong influence, however, and don't give it much attention.

In an apartment, the "front door" is the door that leads from the shared/public spaces of the hallway or courtyard into your private space. All the residents of the building have keys to the front door to the building, but only you have a key to your apartment, so that's the door that determines the *ba gua* of your space.

The guidelines for determining the *ba gua* of your apartment are the same as for a house: place the lower edge of the *ba gua* to line up with the front door, then stretch the *ba gua* to cover the length and width of the apartment, adjusting for any extensions or missing areas.

THE BA GUA FOR A ROOM

The *ba gua* for a room is just like the *ba gua* for a house. Line it up with the doorway and stretch it to cover the room, adjusting for extensions and missing areas as described on the previous pages.

If there is more than one way to enter the room, orient the *ba gua* to the most prominent entryway architecturally. If the entries are equal, choose the one that is used more frequently. If you still aren't sure, use the doorway that opens into the more active area of the home.

Many rooms have missing areas and/or extensions to the outline of the room itself. These only affect the *ba gua* of that particular room. They have no affect on the overall house *ba gua*.

Resources

FastFengShui.com

Our flagship feng shui website offers:

- Information about contemporary Western feng shui
- Extensive Articles and FAQs pages
- Excerpts for all *Fast Feng Shui* books
- Free e-booklets to download
- A multi-vendor resource for feng shui products and accessories—water fountains, wind chimes, lighting, candles, air purifiers and environmental health products, Chinese feng shui cures and accessories and more. We've searched the Internet and found the best.
- Free feng shui newsletter
- Extensive Links and Resources pages providing access to the best of the Internet for feng shui and related topics.

FengShuiEbooks.com

Instant access to the e-book editions of our popular *Fast Feng Shui* books, other digital products not available in bookstores, and free e-booklet feng shui guides.

EMF-Health.com

Information you need to know about the hidden dangers of EMF and microwave pollution and the very real risks they pose to your health. Online videos and research reports, plus the products you need to protect yourself and your family. These are the solutions we use in our own home.

ClutterFreeForever.com

Learn how to liberate yourself from clutter, the *Fast Feng Shui* way!

Index

A

affirmations 21, 229
air quality 54
aquariums 207, 222
art 164-166, 170, 176, 178, 183, 205
astrology 229
attention 35, 176, 178, 184, 221
attic, home office in 53-54, 164
attitude 17, 40, 54, 161, 225, 226

B

ba gua 56, 103, 147, 183-184, 230,
   231, 234
   and clutter 92
   and your occupation 65, 66
   colors of 110, 150, 195
   elements associated with 195-196
   experiential symbolism 63
   grid method 60-62, 193, 239, 248
   meanings of 56-57
   of your desk 56, 218
   "pie slice" method 60-61, 239
   placement of
      compass method 57-58, 64, 244
      doorway method 57, 62, 64,
      248
bamboo 210
bamboo flutes 173-174
basement, home office in 53-54, 165
blessing ceremony 211, 230
Board of Directors, Virtual 215
bookcases 91, 96, 99, 136, 140, 147,
   162, 164, 169, 172, 178
business partnerships 65

C

candles 212, 214, 231
CAREER area 92, 184-185, 207-
   208. See also kan gua
cash flow 90, 139
ceiling fans 137
ceilings
   cathedral 139
   slanted 138, 164, 174
change, embracing 234
chi 37

flow of 15, 77, 89, 115, 149-155,
   157, 163, 175-178, 183
path of 33-34, 151, 172
personal 132-134, 166, 222
predecessor 32
stale or stagnant 91, 149
stale, removing 86
chien gua 57, 94, 190-191, 214-216
childcare 98
children 94, 190, 213-214. See also
   dui gua
clocks 102, 217, 222
closets 90-91, 95, 102
clutter 29, 39, 53, 85, 87, 89-90, 94-
   99, 101, 104, 106, 117, 145-146,
   151, 155, 163, 168, 171, 175, 183,
   214, 217
   and the ba gua 92
coins 210-211
collage 206, 218
command position 34-35, 125-126,
   128, 130, 132, 143, 145, 148,
   163. See also desk: positioning
   for desk 130-131
   within the home 50
communication 103
COMMUNITY area 57, 186, 205, 209-
   210
compass, how to read 245
computers 103, 105
CREATIVITY area 54, 89-90, 94, 190,
   205, 213, 214. See also dui gua
crystal balls, faceted 15, 36, 161, 169,
   172, 177-178, 205, 212, 214-217
crystals, natural 164, 173, 214-216
curtains 169, 173, 177,-178

D

depression 54, 135, 139, 149
desk 116
   as symbol of your business 116-
      117, 120, 145
   condition of 25, 32, 102, 118
   elements represented 122
   material made of 121
   positioning 26, 33, 115, 125, 127-

131, 143, 156, 164, 171-174, 183
criteria for 125-126, 143-144
in shared office 128-129, 145
shape of 118-120
size of 32, 117
desk chair 37, 87, 102, 123. *See also* seating
dispelling mudra 228, 233
doors 95, 102, 150, 152-153, 155, 176
dui gua 57, 94, 190, 213, 214

E

EARTH element 164, 165, 208, 213-215, 217
electro-magnetic fields (EMF) 54, 140-141, 148, 174, 246
element interactions
Controlling cycle 200, 202
Creative cycle 197-202, 205, 207
Reducing cycle 198, 200, 202
elements 163, 179, 183, 196, 201, 204-205, 217, 222
and the *ba gua* 195, 201-202
colors of 121, 195, 197
materials 121, 197
qualities of 121, 124
represented by your desk 122
shapes of 121, 197
email 29, 38
EMF. *See* electro-magnetic fields
EMF-health.com 140-142, 174
employees 57, 190, 214
empowerment, IVAG 228-229
exposed beams 138, 173
extensions. *See* floor plan: extensions

F

fabric 168, 174, 213, 230
FAME area 57, 60, 118, 184, 188-189, 212
FAMILY area 57, 95, 186, 209
Fast Feng Shui 16, 184
fatigue 17, 135, 140, 149, 172
feng shui
benefits of 9
contemporary western 15, 62
eight mansions 16

flying stars method 11, 16
overview of 10
figurines 172, 231
filing 97, 99
FIRE element 208, 212, 213, 214, 216
floor plans 44
compass sectors of 60
extensions 193-194, 252
how to draw 237-238
irregularly shaped spaces 75-76, 78, 168-169, 241, 252
missing areas 78, 168-169, 193-194, 252
flowers 37-38, 207, 209, 212-217, 222, 230
artificial 38
focal points 28, 37, 170, 175, 219, 221
fortunate blessings 188, 210, 233. *See also* WEALTH area, *hsun gua.*
front door, proximity to 49-50
furniture 115, 155, 177, 213
used 32, 116

G

goals 89, 183-185, 186, 192, 234
goldfish 210, 222
gratitude 228-229
guardian figures 172

H

hallways 95, 151
headaches 138, 140
health 57, 95, 133, 135, 139, 140, 141, 163, 191
HELPFUL FRIENDS area 94, 190, 214-215. *See also chien gua*
home office
as microcosm of business 18, 145
chi of 53, 101, 106, 153-155, 161, 166, 196, 201
in the bedroom 52, 148
in the dining room 145-146
in the living room 146-147
location of 45, 61, 162, 183
pros and cons compared 79
size of 77-78, 170-171
unsuitable locations 52, 164-165
Home Office Assessment 25

housekeeping 29, 38, 83, 86, 91, 101, 102, 104
hsun gua 56, 184, 187-188, 210, 233

I

imagery 15, 37, 91, 164, 174, 205-206, 216, 218, 222
incense 230
inspiration 103, 108, 115, 149, 206
integrity, acting with 17, 40
intention 15, 184, 191, 225-229
intuition 118

J

jen gua 57, 186-187, 210
journal, keeping a 21

K

kan gua 57, 60, 92, 184-185, 207-208
karma 18
ken gua 57, 92, 186, 208, 209
KNOWLEDGE area. *See ken gua*
kua number 68, 166
kun gua 57, 94, 189, 213

L

li gua 57, 60, 184, 188, 212
Life Aspirations 56,184, 192, 234.
   See also ba gua: meanings of
lighting 30, 39, 53, 73, 103, 111, 164-66, 170, 174, 208, 212, 214
luck 18
lucky directions 12, 16, 61, 68, 125, 126, 148, 173
   east and west groups 70, 128
   floor plan sectors 71, 166
   for desk position 127-129, 143, 166
   kua numbers 68-69

M

mail 29, 38, 104
mantra 228
marriage 189, 213
Mastermind Group 190
meditation 191
mentors 57, 94, 190
METAL element 207, 209, 213, 214, 216
mirrors 73, 168, 171-172, 175,-178, 207. *See also* remedies
missing areas. *See* floor plan: missing areas
mixed-use spaces 47, 87, 98, 150-151, 162
mobiles 165, 209, 222
money tree 210
mood 30, 40, 54, 90, 221
"mouth of *chi*" 62, 150

N

network marketing 94, 187, 190, 206, 214
networking 90

O

occupations 65-66
office location and profession 54
opportunities 15, 38, 39, 85, 89, 90, 102, 149, 152

P

paint 53, 85, 87, 106, 108, 150
   color selection tips 111
partnerships 189, 213. *See kun gua*, RELATIONSHIPS area
personal growth 186
photographs 111, 163-166, 213, 222
plants 28, 37, 38, 49, 50, 147, 162, 164-166, 169-170, 172, 174, 177, 178, 209, 210, 215, 222. *See also* remedies
plastic 204
power spots 15, 38, 184, 193, 194, 196, 201, 205, 206, 211, 217, 219, 220
prayer 228
predecessor *chi* 85, 116
productivity 99, 115
prosperity 117, 205, 210, 211

Q

Quick Fix Solutions 32

R

recognition 91, 188

red envelopes 231
RELATIONSHIPS area 89, 94, 189, 213. *See also kun gua*
remedies 15, 89, 161, 183, 225
REPUTATION area 188-189, 212. *See also li gua*
rice 211, 231
room shape. *See* floor plan

S

screen, as room divider 49, 147, 162, 170, 177
seating 28, 37
secret arrows 36, 76, 133, 134, 135, 142, 164, 169, 173, 212
  causes of 136
  factors affecting impact 137
sha chi 36, 76, 78, 125-126, 131, 134-135, 142-143, 145, 148, 161, 164, 166, 169, 173, 212
  and desk position 76, 142
  EMF 140-142, 148
  oppressive 133, 138-140, 142, 148, 164, 166
shared workspace 13
sound 168, 207, 212-213
spirituality 57, 186, 209
storage 90, 91, 96, 98, 99, 146, 148, 155, 164, 165, 168, 169, 171
stress 30, 34, 48, 89, 95, 97, 99, 131, 133, 139, 149, 151, 157, 191, 217
success 117, 186, 188, 205, 226
symbols 37, 183, 205, 206, 221, 225, 226, 227

T

tai chi 48, 57, 95, 163, 191, 216-217, 234
  center of the *ba gua* 56
"Tracing the 9-Star Path" 230
TRAVEL area 94, 190-191, 214, 216. *See also chien gua*

V

vision 103, 188
visualization 21, 227, 229, 231
vitality 37, 204, 222

W

wall color 73, 106-108, 111, 147, 162, 201
  and the *ba gua* 110
  emotional impact of 109
WATER element 207, 209, 210, 216
water fountains 169, 205, 207, 222
WEALTH area 56, 57, 184, 187, 188, 210, 211. *See also hsun gua.*
wind chimes 15, 205, 210
windows 36, 54, 103, 152, 153, 154, 155, 165, 175, 178
WOOD element 164, 209, 210, 212
work habits 39

Y

yin and *yang* attributes of a space 72-74
  adjustments for 166-168
yoga 191

About the Author

Stephanie Roberts is the author of the acclaimed *Fast Feng Shui* book series, the *Clutter-Free Forever! Home Coaching Program* (soon to be available in book format as *Clutter-Clearing from the Inside Out*), and *The Pocket Idiot's Guide to Feng Shui*.

A native New Englander, Stephanie graduated *magna com laude* from Harvard with a degree in Art History. Throughout the 1980s and 90s, Stephanie lived in New York City, where she had a successful career developing training seminars and self-instructional materials for major corporations.

A long-time student of metaphysics, Stephanie shifted her focus in the mid-1990s to the study and practice of contemporary western feng shui. In 1999, after applying feng shui to her own life, she ended her corporate career and moved to Hawaii with her future husband, FastFengShui.com webmaster Taraka Serrano.

Stephanie and Taraka now dedicate their lives to writing and publishing books about feng shui and related topics, and, through their websites, guiding others to release limitation, reach new levels of health and wellbeing, and realize the life of their dreams... just like they have!